Hal Sigurdson

Bob Picken

STEVE PATRICK

BLUE & GOLD

BLUE & GOLD

75 YEARS OF BLUE BOMBER GLORY

EDITED BY BOB IRVING

Great Plains Publications
420 – 70 Arthur Street
Winnipeg, MB R3B 1G7
www.greatplains.mb.ca

Great Plains Publications gratefully acknowledges the financial support provided for its publishing program by the Government of Canada through the Book Publishing Industry Development Program (BPIDP); the Canada Council for the Arts; as well as the Manitoba Department of Culture, Heritage and Tourism; and the Manitoba Arts Council.

Design & Typography by Relish Design Studio Ltd.

Printed in Canada by Friesens Printing

CANADIAN CATALOGUING IN PUBLICATION DATA

Main entry under title:

Blue & gold : 75 years of Blue Bomber history / edited by Bob Irving.

ISBN 1-894283-59-7

Winnipeg Blue Bombers (Football team)—History. I. Irving, Bob, 1950-
II. Title: Blue and gold.

GV948.3.W55B58 2005 796.335'64'09712743 C2005-903320-7

■ Kenny Ploen and Dieter Brock as Butch Cassidy and the Sundance Kid.

MESSAGE FROM THE PREMIER

On behalf of the citizens and government of the Province of Manitoba, it is indeed a pleasure to extend hearty congratulations to the players, coaches and fans of the Winnipeg Football Club on the occasion of your 75th Anniversary!

From the beginning, Manitobans have been passionate about their football club, and its fortunes on and off the field. With a record of ten Grey Cup victories, fans have not been disappointed. The Blue Bombers have also become well-known for their commitment to community service as well as athleticism.

It is important to note that the lessons learned on the gridiron translate into important life lessons – the significance of teamwork, dedication and hard work.

Congratulations again, Blue Bombers. Here's looking at another 75 more years of great football!

GARY DOER
Premier of Manitoba

MESSAGE FROM THE MINISTER

Congratulations on 75 Years of Blue Bomber Glory!

As Manitoba's Minister of Culture, Heritage and Tourism and Minister responsible for Sport, it is my great pleasure to congratulate the Winnipeg Blue Bombers Football Club on 75 years of excellence in sports. The Bombers are an important sports icon for our province, a team all Manitobans take great pride in supporting.

Over the years, the football club has evolved into one of the best teams in the Canadian league and many Bombers have provided exceptional role models for our young athletes. The team's longevity in the CFL speaks volumes about the ongoing quality of the club's players, coaches and managers, as well as the loyalty of the fans.

Having a thriving CFL team in Manitoba is not only great for provincial pride, it's also great for tourism and I wish the Blue Bombers many years of continued success.

ERIC ROBINSON
Minister of Culture, Heritage and Tourism
Minister responsible for Sport

MESSAGE FROM THE MAYOR

Whether you are involved in sports, entertainment, construction, finance, retail, or yes, even in politics, 75 years is a long time to be in any business. But during those seven decades, our city has consistently been able to cheer for the Blue and Gold.

Winnipeg has been blessed to have such a fantastic sports organization in our city. The Winnipeg Football Club has been a great source of pride and entertainment for Winnipeg and all of Manitoba. Your longevity in the Canadian Football League speaks for itself and is a testament to the fans across Manitoba and the strong fan base and community you have developed over the years.

And like I said, Winnipeggers will have the opportunity to thank you for 75 years of high calibre sports next year when we host the 2006 Grey Cup. Because as your organization has long known, and was proven at the Junos earlier this year, nobody knows how to party like Winnipeggers.

I also want to commend all the Bomber alumni who have provided us with years of lasting memories. It is your passion, dedication, and spirit, that has allowed the Bombers to be a hallmark of the CFL and our wonderful city.

Thank you very much for all you do, and keep up the great work.

SAM KATZ
Mayor of Winnipeg

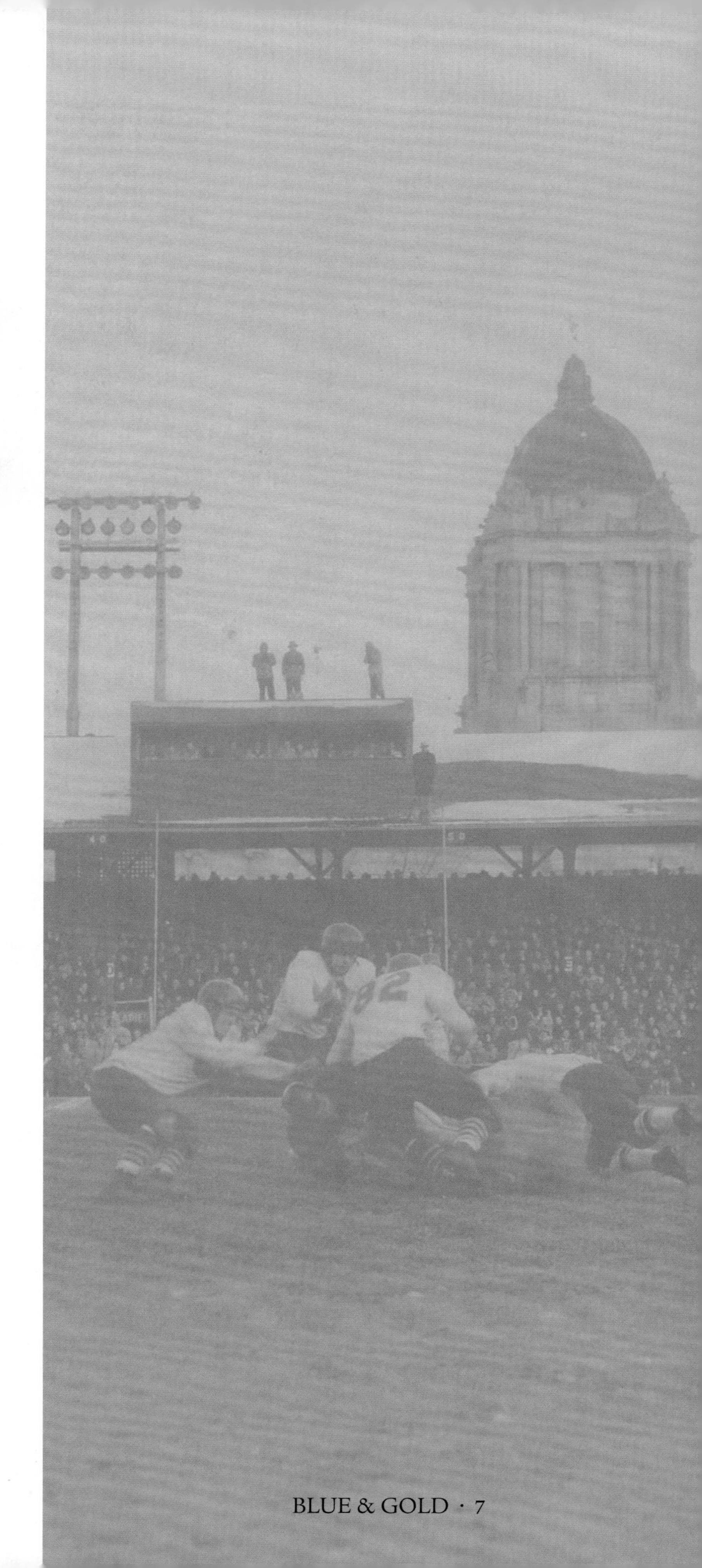

Riddell
RONA
CFL

CONTENTS

Dave Darichuk

FOREWORD

BY PAUL ROBSON

Former player / General Manager
Winnipeg Blue Bombers

Any institution that survives 75 years accumulates with it certain myths, facts and fantasies. The contributors to this retrospective of the history of the Winnipeg Football Club will try to dispel the myths, catalogue the facts and maintain the fantasies that surround and amplify the story of a truly unique relationship between a province, a city and a football team.

Having begun my 52-year journey with the Winnipeg Football Club in the summer of 1953, I have the advantage of a unique point of view as a player, as a manager and, as the following story illustrates, as a fan.

In the summer of 1953, Ralph Misener was the president of the Blue Bombers and I was his paper boy at Whytewold Beach. To my great surprise he invited me to accompany his sons to the Bombers season opener in the newly constructed Winnipeg Stadium—Tom Casey, Neil Armstrong, Lorne Benson, Keith Pearce, Tommy Ford, Jack Jacobs—I was hooked on Bomber football!

But how was I going to get to see more?

Somehow word got to Mr. Misener that I wanted to go to more games; so he agreed to drive me in to another game where he introduced me to Johnny Peterson, the general manager of the newly created Winnipeg Enterprises. The end result was a job selling popcorn for Ed Corbeil. I got to go to all the games that year. What a great job, I got to see my heroes play and went home with $5 to $10 each game—I was hooked on Bomber football!... Again!

That's the way it started for me. For thousands of other Manitobans, somehow, something happens that hooks us on the unique experience of Blue Bomber football.

What is the catalyst that has melded the Football Club into the everyday fabric of the community and made it as much a part of us as Portage and Main or the Golden Boy?

Maybe it is because the Winnipeg Football Club has always been led by the most able of the community's business and professional men and women. From G. Sydney Halter and Arthur U. Chipman to Neville Winograd, David Asper and Gene Dunn, the Blue Bombers have attracted the best.

Maybe it is because so many of the players came up through the amateur ranks in Winnipeg...the Rods, the Wildcats, the Winnipeg Light Infantry, the Rams. And maybe it is because so many of them, Canadian and American, made their homes in Manitoba. From Mel Wilson and Andy Bieber to Nick Miller, Steve Patrick, Cornel Piper, Ed Kotowich and Ken Ploen to Joe Poplawski and Chris Walby, all have been accessible to the community and a part of its daily life.

Maybe it is because some of Canada's most talented writers and broadcasters have covered the Blue and Gold—Jim Coleman, Stew McPherson, Maurice Smith, Hal Sigurdson, Jack Matheson and the incomparable Cactus Jack Wells. Their legends remain for the current crop of ink-stained wretches and breathless prognosticators to emulate.

Maybe it is because the Canadian game of football as played by the Bombers has always been exciting, wide-open, hard-hitting and reflective of what we as Manitobans cherish in ourselves.

Maybe it is because the Bombers have had such excellent coaching staffs—from Reg Threlfall to Bud Grant to Cal Murphy to Mike Riley or because of such legendary backs as Fritz Hanson, Jack Jacobs, Gerry James, Leo Lewis, Ken Ploen, Don Jonas, Dieter Brock, Tom Clements, Willard Reaves and Matt Dunigan.

Maybe it is because certain Blue Bomber memories become more sharply defined as images of our youth: Hudson Bay's Junior Quarterback Club meetings, the Salisbury House Kids Section, Cliff Gardner and the Bomber Boosters 'Hang Down Your Head Jim Trimble', Ticats/Bombers Grey Cups.

Maybe all of this is why the Winnipeg Football Club has endured through 75 years of community ownership; reflecting and defining our image of ourselves as a community. It's more than a game, it's more than a team, it's a lifelong relationship that revives every summer and flourishes through the fall until we arrive triumphant or heartbroken in November to endure another winter in Winnerpeg! ■

Ken Gigliotti, Winnipeg Free Press

PREFACE

BY DAVID ASPER

Former President of the Winnipeg Blue Bombers

"Dad, we really need some DB's," said my son for the one-thousandth time. "Daniel, coverage is a function of the whole defence and not just a single position," I replied for the one-thousandth time.

It's April and talk of football is revived in my home. Changing the clocks forward is like flicking the switch, and it's been like that ever since I was a kid nagging my father just like my own kids do today. We are like bears awakening from our sleep. Ready to start hunting for Lions, Tiger Cats, Alouettes, Roughriders and definitely Eskimos. Out come the jerseys, tattered t-shirts and scratched up J5-V's.

The ritual started with my parents who conveniently arranged to have me born in November 1958 as the Bombers won the Grey Cup that year. From that moment my dad and his brother made me a fan, and Winnipeg has been blessed by the fact that our family enclave is but one of thousands who have played such an important role in the success and history of the Blue Bombers.

I was too young to remember the Bud Grant glory years, and accordingly, suffered through the 22-year drought leading up to the '84 pounding of Hamilton at Commonwealth Stadium. That era was when the big lesson got taught. Win, lose or draw, if you are a fan, be a fan and don't pretend. It was a lesson in life about loyalty and never losing sight of the dream, whether it is a Grey Cup victory or your own goals in life.

In '84, all Bomber fans changed our shared common experience of losing. As Paul Robson said at the time, our winter became warmer that year. We were Winnerpeggers. Then came '88 and '90. As the Bud Grant years were to my father, the Cal Murphy/Mike Riley years are to me.

My first child was born in 1990. Cal Murphy nearly fainted when my wife was in early labour and there we were, walking, as the doctor suggested, around the stadium watching practice. Twelve days later, the newest Asper saw his first Bomber home game as we beat Toronto 34-17. Over the next four years my wife and I created two more future season ticket holders, and in so doing, we have maintained the circle started by my dad.

A few days after my father passed away, the Bombers had a home game scheduled. It was a difficult time, but I figured he would want me to go. After the game Coach Ritchie and the team gave our family a game ball. It's a cherished possession and a fitting symbol for me to hand off to the next generation of Blue Bomber fans.

Life can sometimes be difficult. When it is, I find simplicity and solace in two words: Go Bombers. ■

■ Robert Mimbs and Rick House: *Time to celebrate.*

INTRODUCTION

BY BOB IRVING

LGIW. That's what my dear friend Jack Matheson called his wife Peggy when he was making his magic with the *Winnipeg Tribune* as one of the greatest wordsmiths in the history of Canadian sports journalism. It stood for "luckiest girl in the world," and those letters, LGIW, could easily be transposed into how I feel about having had the pleasure of covering the Winnipeg Blue Bombers for the past 32 years. If I'm not the "luckiest guy in the world" I don't know who is.

It all started in 1973, shortly after a chance meeting with the late Ken "The Friar" Nicolson in the parking lot of the Clear Lake Golf Course resulted in me being hired by CJOB. My lifelong dream had come true. I was going to get a chance to be a fulltime sports broadcaster. Little did I know what excitement was ahead. The Friar immediately threw me into the role of hosting the

■ (From left) Joe Turner, Don Smith, Marvin Bergson, Frank Zajac, 1946: *When we were kings.*

Western Canada Pictorial Index

■ Quarterback Ken Ploen: *Four Grey Cup championships and a member of the Canadian Football Hall of Fame.*

Winnipeg Blue Bomber post-game show from the Carling O'Keefe trailer across the road from the stadium. To my right was the legendary Ken Ploen, to my left, recently retired tight end Mitch Zalnasky. It was a bit overwhelming, but it was also an indescribable thrill for a cub reporter from Regina via Estevan and Brandon, for someone who had grown up loving the CFL and worshipping at the Taylor Field shrine of Ronnie and George (that would be Lancaster and Reed) and those outstanding Saskatchewan teams of the 1960s. I will be forever grateful to Ken and Mitch for carrying me during those early days when my experience was limited but my enthusiasm was boundless.

In 1974, when the Friar decided he didn't have time to do play-by-play of both the Blue Bombers and the Winnipeg Jets, he turned the football play-by-play over to me. So, here I was, at the age of 24, the youngest of the nine CFL play-by-play announcers. And before long I was sharing the microphone with Ploen and Zalnasky and Matty and Cactus Jack Wells. Joining me as colour commentators in later years were Joe Poplawski and Geoff Currier. Even when CJOB lost the broadcast rights during the 1980s, our commitment to Bomber coverage never waned as I travelled with the team throughout each season.

Very early in my days at CJOB I developed an understanding and appreciation of how

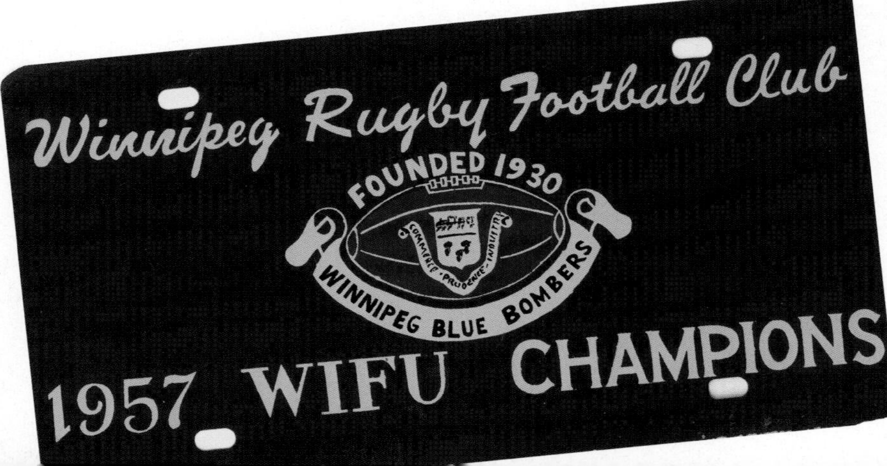

much the Winnipeg Football Club meant to the city, how deeply connected so many thousands of citizens were to the Blue Bombers. To say the last 32 years have been a labour of love would be a gross understatement. I look back on my time covering the Bombers with overwhelming feelings of fondness, not to mention emotion. From the days of Earl Lunsford, Jim Spavital and Don Jonas through the Paul Robson-Cal Murphy era, into the tumultous times of Jeff Reinebold, and the resurgence of the Lyle Bauer-Dave Ritchie-Brendan Taman period, I have cherished every moment of covering a team that is so very relevant to the lives of so many people.

My name has been linked, however superficially, with one of the great franchises in Canadian sports history. And now, I have been asked to play a role in crafting this book during which we relive the rich 75-year history and tradition of the Winnipeg Blue Bombers. Thanks to Trevor Kennerd of the Bomber Alumni and Gregg Shilliday of Great Plains Publications for the invitation, thanks to the chapter and sidebar writers and to everyone who played a role in making this book happen. The pleasure has been all mine. As Matty would say, that makes me the LGIW. ■

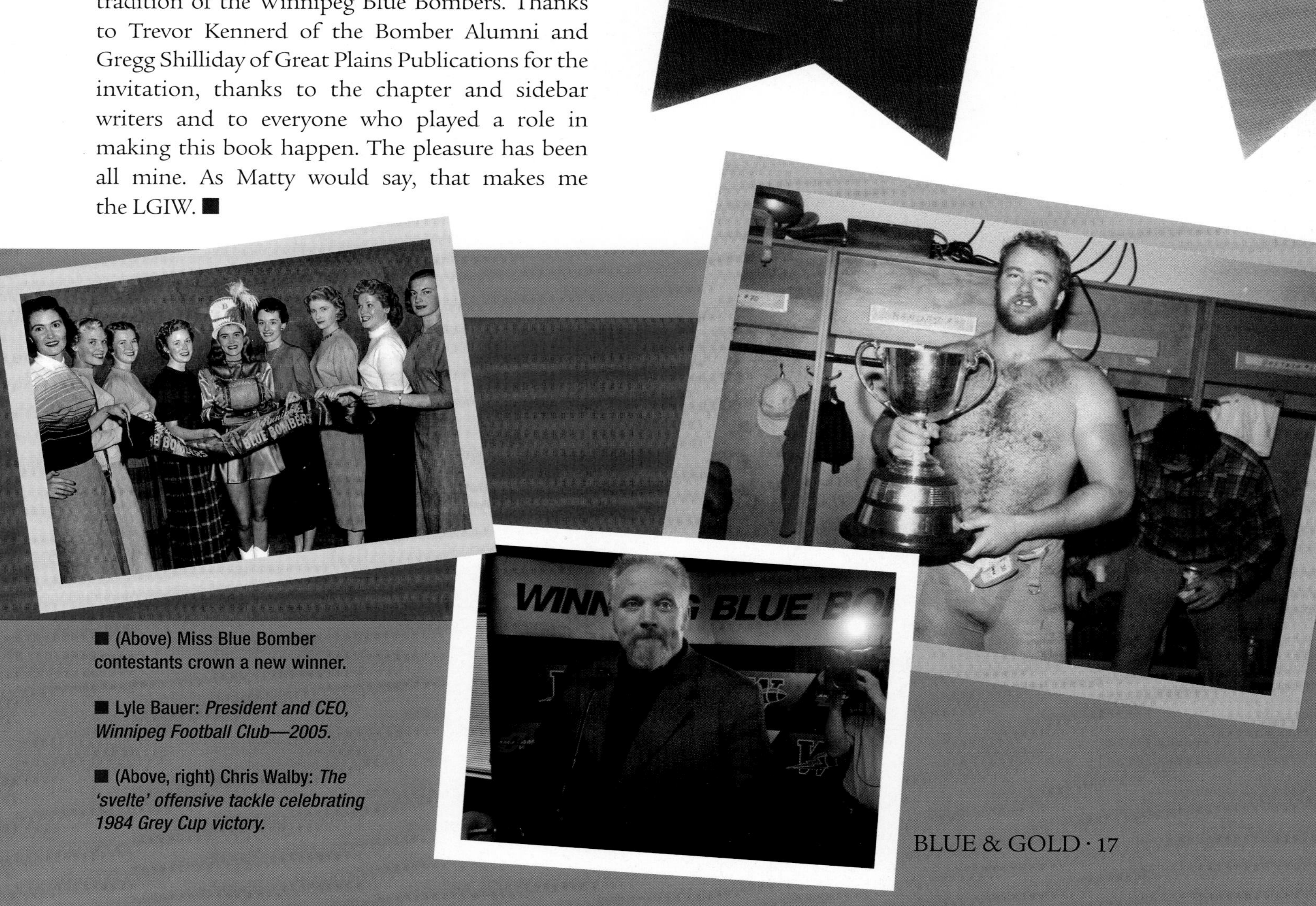

■ (Above) Miss Blue Bomber contestants crown a new winner.

■ Lyle Bauer: *President and CEO, Winnipeg Football Club—2005.*

■ (Above, right) Chris Walby: *The 'svelte' offensive tackle celebrating 1984 Grey Cup victory.*

CHAPTER 1

Western Canada Pictorial Index

■ The 'Galloping Ghost,' Fritz Hanson: *Led Blue Bombers to 1935 Grey Cup with a record 300 yards in punt returns.*

THE EARLY YEARS

BY HAL SIGURDSON

Life wasn't easy for the team now known as the Winnipeg Blue Bombers when it sprang to life in 1930 as a member of the recently created Western Interprovincial Football Union. Then again, give or take the odd rum-runner, life wasn't easy for anyone in the era known as the "Dirty Thirties."

The Depression was less than a year old when teams from Winnipeg, Regina, Edmonton, and Calgary—a Vancouver team alternately known as Meralomas or Grizzlies was sometimes included—combined to form the old WIFU. The league's goals were to improve the quality of play in western Canada and mount a legitimate challenge for the Grey Cup. Well, legitimate enough to make those eastern toffs lose their smirks when they showed up to play.

■ Osborne Stadium 1935: *The first 'snow bowl'.*

Archives of Manitoba

It is impossible to exaggerate the hardship of that era. The future seemed so bleak we kept hearing reports that members of the formerly rich were ending it all with a long step off a tall building. The unemployed boarded empty freight cars to search for jobs farther down the line only to discover there weren't any jobs there, either. Knowing thousands of other people were in the same fix offered extremely cold comfort.

Then, as if trying to launch a new team in those days wasn't hard enough, members had to endure its first three years of existence known as the "Winnipeg Winnipegs."

Yikes!

ORIGINS OF THE GAME

A search of the archives reveals Winnipeggers have been watching—and playing—a hybrid version of a game that evolved from a mix of soccer, rugby and football since 1870. Indeed, popular legend takes it back further still. If you want to find someone to blame you can lay it all on the confused head of a young man named William Webb Ellis.

Why him? As Sherlock Holmes would have put it: "Elementary my dear Watson."

Westerners wanted to liberalize the blocking rules and "open up" the game. Easterners, still wearing old school ties, kept dismissing these requests as "Americanization."

We are told that in 1823 young Webb Ellis was attending Rugby, the famous British school. On the day alleged to have changed history we learn this young man was playing a game known as football on his side of the Atlantic but frequently called soccer on ours. Could this story get more confusing? Yes it could. And it did.

Young William's mind must have been somewhere else when the ball came whizzing toward him chin high early in the second half. Instead of heading it or playing it off his body he chose to catch the darn thing and run toward the opposing team's goal line. The referee was not amused and wasted no time in ejecting young

■ Osborne Stadium, circa 1938.

Manitoba Sports Hall of Fame

Webb Ellis. However, there were a few people in the stands who were not nearly as offended by the young man's unorthodox maneuver as the referee. On the contrary they thought a game where players could pick up the ball and run with it as well as kick it might have a future.

And so it has. The game now known as rugby or rugger is still alive and well in most of the world's English speaking nations. In North America, however, the game chose a different path. In The United States it was a 90-degree turn and became the four-down game still played in the National Football League and most college campuses. Canadians, typically, chose a more gradual evolution.

In its earliest days football in Canada was governed by a body known as the CRU, short for the Canadian Rugby Union. Since many of its members were Ontarians descended from ancestors who chose to move north rather than take part in the American revolution of 1776, they

REG THRELFALL: INSTILLING A WINNING TRADITION

BY BOB IRVING

Reg Threlfall was one of the winningest coaches in the Bombers' early years. He succeeded Bob Fritz as coach of the Blue and Gold in 1938. Threlfall, a native of Newton, Massachusetts, attended Purdue University and came to the Bombers after serving as head football coach and athletic director at South Dakota State. From 1938 through 1941, Threlfall's Bomber teams won 28 regular season games and lost only eight while making it to three Grey Cups, winning twice over Ottawa in 1939 and 1941 and losing to the Toronto Argonauts in 1938.

With World War Two raging, the Blue Bombers didn't actually play any games in 1942 and 1943, but Threlfall presided over a senior league sponsored by the Bombers that was designed to keep football alive. Despite the war, the Grey Cup game was played both those years, and one of those Winnipeg senior teams, the RCAF Bombers, played in and lost the Cup in both '42 and '43.

Threlfall left football in 1944 to work fulltime in the insurance business. Blue Bomber historian and former *Winnipeg Tribune* columnist Vince Leah gave Threlfall credit for advising Blue Bomber coach Bud Sherman in 1953 to sign a player named Bud Grant, who would go on to gain legendary status as a coach with the Bombers. Leah said Threlfall was colourful and friendly, one of the most popular football personalities ever to come to Winnipeg. Reg Threlfall passed away in February of 1971.

Western Canada Pictorial Index

■ **Head Coach Reg Threlfall:** ***Two-time Grey Cup champion, 1939 & 1941.***

Bob Irving is the sports director for CJOB 68 Radio.

weren't nearly as eager to follow the Americans' lead as were the impatient westerners. The result is eastern and western Canadians have been bickering over the rules of the game for nearly 100 years. That Webb Ellis kid has a lot to answer for.

Westerners wanted to liberalize the blocking rules and "open up" the game. Easterners, still wearing old school ties, kept dismissing these requests as "Americanization." Believe it or not we are told that westerners became so outraged by the inflexible stance of the CRU there was talk of separation. Sound familiar? Nothing came of it, of course, but rules were still a subject of angry debate as late the Bud Grant era (1957-66). Every now and then they still are.

But back to the "Winnipeg Winnipegs" who didn't stop repeating themselves until 1934. Even then it wasn't as the result of any carefully researched and thought-out executive decision. In fact, the Bombers owe their merciful name change to an old sports writer fondly remembered by all as "Uncle Vince."

■ **Journalist and author Vince Leah:** ***The man who named the team.***

■ Game action from 1935: *Russ Rebholtz scoring a touchdown.*

Western Canada Pictorial Index

Vince Leah worked at the old *Winnipeg Tribune* almost forever. When the *Trib* folded he went to work for the *Winnipeg Free Press* without missing a beat. Earlier in his career, however, he became impressed by the exploits of Joe Louis, for many years the champion of boxing's heavyweight division. As his fame grew Lewis became known as "The Brown Bomber."

Today that title probably wouldn't make it past the language police, but Uncle Vince thought it had a nice ring to it. Like most people of the era, he didn't much care for the repetitive "Winnipeg Winnipegs" handle. Since the Winnipegs had recently adopted blue uniforms, he decided calling them the "Blue Bombers" would be a big step forward. It was. Not much later club officers agreed and made the name change official.

As previously noted five cities held membership in the old Western Inter-provincial Football Union in 1930, at least off and on. However, what subsequent generations appear to have forgotten is individual cities, including Winnipeg, sometimes had more than one team. A team had to win the city title before it could advance to inter-provincial play and a shot at the Grey Cup. The Garrison, staffed mostly with players and management from the military, was seldom a serious threat. St. John's, on the other hand, consistently gave the future Blue Bombers all they could handle and more, and in 1932, St. John's bested the "Winnipegs" and advanced to the western Canada semi-finals where they lost 9-1 to the Regina Roughriders.

The year 1932 marked the real start of professionalism in Winnipeg football. St. Johns brought in Russ Rebholz from the University of Wisconsin to be their quarterback and coach, and they also recruited all-American end Bud Reiger. Throw in Canadians Eddie James, Tom Mobberly and Steve and Al Olander, and St. Johns had a powerful backfield. The Winnipegs hired Carl Cronin from Notre Dame to be their coach, quarterback and place kicker.

Western Canada Pictorial Index

■ **Blue Bomber player-coach Carl Cronin:** ***The team's head coach, quarter-back and placekicker, 1932-33.***

In 1933 St. John's and the Winnipeg's agreed to a long overdue merger. All-American defensive lineman Greg Kabat joined Cronin and Rebholz to give the Winnipegs an outstanding team that won the Manitoba senior championship and also defeated Regina and Calgary before falling short in their Grey Cup bid by losing 13-0 to the Toronto Argos in a semi-final game. The merger allowed the Winnipegs to get Osborne Stadium, with nearly 6,000 seats, as their home field.

■ **The cold never bothered Bomber fans:** ***Especially with a cigarette to keep you warm.***

But there was a catch. The Johnnies, as they were known, subsidized their Osborne Stadium rental by periodically dispatching players to help manager Johnny (The Great Dane) Petersen apply a new coat of paint to his weather beaten stands. After the merger Winnipegs' players were also handed paint brushes.

However a far stronger motive for merger was supplied by the Saskatchewan Roughriders. Though Regina was only one quarter the size of Winnipeg, the Roughies kept cleaning the clocks of the Manitoba champions in inter-provincial play. Al Ritchie, their silver-tongued recruiter, was remarkably adept at luring talented American players over the border to suit up with the Roughies.

Winnipeg manager Joe Ryan had envied St. John's and their bigger park for years before their eventual merger was completed. After the deal was done, however, he discovered it didn't make his life much easier. These were still the "Dirty Thirties," remember. If football players could be recruited for room and board and the promise of an off-field job, guess how many people could afford to buy season tickets.

Nevertheless, it all turned out pretty well. Old Wesley Park is now real estate occupied by the University of Winnipeg. Osborne Stadium was replaced by Winnipeg Stadium in 1953. Great West Life is now headquartered on the land it once occupied.

■ **Ed Bilski, Les Lear, Jack 'Duke' Manners, Albert 'Ole' Olsen, Cliff Roseborough:** ***At Osborne Stadium, 1943***

Western Canada Pictorial Index

Before the merger, city-based teams would play one another two or three times a season. Then they would try to arrange several exhibition games against college competition in North Dakota or Minnesota. That helped both teams on several counts. For one thing they needed the additional competition. For another it was a good way to scout future U.S. talent. Finally their thrifty general managers discovered football equipment was cheaper in North Dakota and Minnesota than at home.

SURVIVING ON A SHOE STRING

Thrift was the key to football's survival in the '30s, pre-merger and after. While St. John's was easing its rental costs with unpaid painters, the Bombers' Ryan responded with his own cost-saving strategy. After a game with St. John's played in a rain storm on the grassless, mud field of Wesley Park Ryan took his own cost-saving measure. He loaded every mud-caked uniform into his car, took them home and washed them by hand. When the sun finally came out he hung the whole sodden mess over his back fence. It's hard to picture Lyle Bauer topping that act.

After the merger Ryan would admit his Winnipegs were often unable to fill all the seats they had in their old Wesley Park home. No matter. It had other, far more endearing qualities as the late Jim Coleman—one of the most widely read sports writers this country has ever produced—revealed in his book, *Long Ride on a Hobby Horse*. Indeed, Wesley Park was the key ingredient in what must still rank as one of the most inventive family enterprises in Manitoba history.

Brother Lou Mogul was a centre and a staunch member of the Winnipegs' line. Meanwhile, sister Fanny Mogul operated a highly successful bootlegging establishment from the third floor of a building directly across the street from the field. A large window offered a splendid view of the action. On cold and/or rainy nights Ryan was often heard to complain more people had watched his games from Fanny's window than from Wesley Park's seats.

Today's sports fans could credibly argue Fanny was simply a few decades ahead of her time. Now well-heeled business firms pay upwards of $100,000 a season to reward good customers and important business associates with glassed-in box seats to major sporting events. Once inside guests are free to consume all the good food and strong drink they can handle. Not only is all this perfectly legal, government encourages the practice. The firms who buy them are allowed to write off their costs as a legitimate business expense called "sales and promotion." If Fanny were alive today she probably would be entitled to a sizeable tax refund.

Future Canadian football legend Fritzie Hanson eventually accepted the deal offered by Winnipeg's Ryan and his gifts were soon putting bottoms into stadium seats wherever he played.

Thrift remained an essential ingredient of every enterprise throughout the '30s, but it became marginally less urgent for the Winnipegs in 1933 following their merger with St. John's. Two years later, when they had established their identity as the Uncle Vince christened Blue Bombers, the always cost-conscious Ryan struck pure gold. He signed his very own superstar—a player with matinee idol good looks and an abundance of talent ideally suited to Canadian football. Future Canadian football legend Fritzie Hanson eventually accepted the deal offered by Winnipegs Ryan and his gifts were soon putting bottoms into stadium seats wherever he played. He also helped create the intense East-West rivalries that define the Grey Cup. The game, no longer a foregone conclusion, now ranks as Canadian sports' most intense event—to say nothing of a week-long party.

Consider this comparison. In the 1935 Grey Cup game where Hanson made his national debut, attendance was reported at 6,405. Gate receipts were entered as $5,583.92. Attendance for the 2004 Grey Cup game was reported as 50,000. Gate receipts weren't reported, but we can safely add

FRITZIE HANSON: THE GALLOPING GHOST

BY HAL SIGURDSON

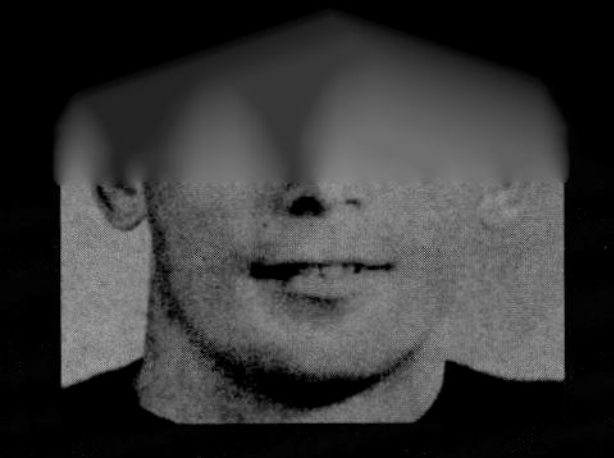

During the Depression years, Canadians needed diversion from the gloom of a failed economy and a menacing climate. Both in movies and sports, people looked for heroes that were larger than life. In Winnipeg, that hero was the "Galloping Ghost."

Fritz Hanson, from Perham, Minnesota, became an instant star in Canadian football of the 1930s. The imaginative sports writers of the day alternated between calling him the "Galloping Ghost," "Twinkle Toes," "the Dipsy Doodle Dandy," or the "Perham Flash."

By any name Hanson was a joy to behold, especially if you were a fan of the Blue Bombers. The icing on the cake was that he was even better than the writers of the day claimed. At only 145 pounds, he was a superb broken field runner and a constant threat on punt returns. On a regular basis he brought the fans who had struggled to find the money for admission jumping to their feet. In his debut year with the Bombers, 1935, he helped the team to their first Grey Cup victory, an 18-12 win over Hamilton.

Hanson played seven seasons in Winnipeg and helped them win the Cup again in 1939 and 1941. He was in his final season in Canada when he collected a fourth Grey Cup ring with the 1948 Calgary Stampeders. Hanson went on to become successful with a Calgary insurance firm after retirement but he will always be remembered as the Bombers' first superstar.

Hal Sigurdson is the former sports editor of the Winnipeg Free Press.

Winnipeg Free Press

Winnipeg Free Press SPORTS NEWS

ZOWIE! 'PEGS WIN

The Day Hanson Dazzled The East

Here's The Team That Made History

Page Prepared By Maurice Smith and Don Blanchard

■ ***Winnipeg Free Press* sports page: *Chronicling 1935 Grey Cup win.***

about four zeros to the 1935 total. As an added bonus the 2004 eastern and western finals drew roughly 50,000 fans apiece and were watched by millions more on television.

Teams have battled for possession of the Grey Cup since 1909 when the University of Toronto defeated a team called Toronto Parkdale, 26-6. In those early years Earl Grey's Cup was almost exclusively an Ontario competition. A western team didn't even get to play until 1921. Unfortunately it didn't play very well. The western champs from Edmonton lost 23-0. In some years the western champion was forced to win a semi-final game with the ORFU (Ontario Rugby Football Union) champion before stepping on the same gridiron as the mighty champions of the Big Four (Montreal, Toronto, Ottawa and Hamilton).

The West found this demeaning but in truth the Big Four's demand wasn't all that unreasonable. The old ORFU produced a lot of competitive teams. In 1936, a year after Hanson's memorable performance, the ORFU Sarnia Imperials won the cup by whipping a team from Ottawa 26-20. Toronto Balmy Beach had won in 1930. In the early days of Grey Cup competition the University of Toronto won it for three straight years beginning in 1909. Queen's University won three in a row beginning in 1922. In one of those years, 1923, they whipped the Regina Roughriders 54-0.

For the next 11 years–three were called off during World War One–the western champs continued to be chopped liver to their eastern rivals. The West was never able to muster more than 12 points in a single game. In fact, the western challenger was blanked twice more after their inauspicious start.

THE GALLOPING GHOST

All that changed in 1935, though there would still a few more bumps to come. It changed because not long after their first meeting in Fargo, Ryan had persuaded Fritz Hanson to play in Winnipeg. Not a big money deal, understand. These were the "Dirty Thirties."

As he would confess many years later, Hanson's rewards included a job with a boss who didn't insist he had to show up for work every day. He also got $125 a game and a subsidy for room and board. That wouldn't be tipping money for today's athletic millionaires but it was big deal in the mid-thirties.

In an era when every American football player from Warroad to the Florida Keys is scouted to within an inch of his life, the Bombers' best financial offer wouldn't have made much of an impression. However, in 1935 most NFL

■ 1935 Bombers on their way to Grey Cup in Toronto: *Best dressed team in the West.*

Archives of Manitoba

■ **Winnipeg Blue Bombers and Osborne Stadium:** ***1939 Grey Cup Champions***

Western Canada Pictorial Index

teams were just as hard pressed for money as their Canadian counterparts. Today's sports agents would laugh at any offer for a star player that included a regular off-field job as an incentive.

When Winnipeg and Hamilton met in the 1935 game the Tigers were fully aware of Hanson's growing reputation. Later they would insist they hadn't taken the Galloping Ghost lightly. On the other hand they couldn't help remembering western teams were winless in 10 previous Grey Cup appearances.

Did the Tigers take the Winnipeg team too lightly? You bet. On that December day in Hamilton, Hanson returned punts for an astonishing 300 yards, still a Cup record. On the other hand, despite Hanson's heroics, the final score was a modest 18-12 and in doubt until the final whistle.

As the years rolled by, opposing coaches kept looking for new strategies to limit his momentum altering punt returns. Frequently this strategy relied on dressing room orations meant to be inspirational. According to popular legend one of those exasperated coaches delivered one that went something like this:

"Listen you guys," he is alleged to have said, "that Hanson is so short (he stood five-foot-six and weighed just 150 pounds) he has to stand on a box to kick a duck in the ass, but game after game you let him make fools of every one of you. You should be ashamed."

History does not record the speech's efficacy, but it fits neatly into the folklore that has built up around Fritzie's storied career. Inspirational speeches were very much in favour during those early days. No one did it better than Regina's affable Al Ritchie, who wound up coaching half the sports organizations in the Regina area. There is no record of his athletic prowess but his verbal skills were legendary.

One of his fiery speeches on a Calgary road trip was overheard through an open window by a member of the opposition. Predictably he returned to his own dressing room and proceeded to repeat all the nasty things Ritchie had to say about them. It may have been the only time in CFL history where one coach provided the pre-game inspiration for both teams.

Many teams have contributed to the game's success, of course. After winning the West, the 1948 Calgary Stampeders' arrived at Toronto's Royal York Hotel with a whole lot more than football players. They were also accompanied by hundreds of party-hungry fans, most of them wearing white hats and driving horse-drawn covered wagons that wound up parked in front of the Royal York. In fact some were even driven into the hotel itself. A lot of football fans who were around in those days have forgotten Calgary defeated Ottawa, 12-7. None has forgotten the party.

The party tradition continues to this day. Most football fans consider that a good thing. It explains why Canadian fans consider their Grey Cup game a lot more fun than the NFL's super-hyped Super Bowl. However, virtually all football fans are agreed no championship game is really worth attending without an element of suspense about the outcome. It was Fritzie Hanson and his rollicking teammates who established that element of doubt.

In truth, however, not quite everyone was swept up in Hanson's spectacular gridiron achievements. Included in that number was Austrian Fritz Kreisler, a world-famous violinist of his time.

In that era football teams always travelled by train. So did world-famous violinists. On the day in question the Bombers were on their way home, celebrating a victory in Calgary's Mewata Stadium.

A few cars away Kreisler and his entourage were headed for their next concert engagement. At some point Hanson's teammates learned Fritz, their esteemed teammate, and Fritz, the esteemed violinist, were on the same train. As the evening progressed it became ever clearer to Hanson's celebrating teammates that two famous men named Fritz simply had to meet.

To sign that group of players at today's prices would be far more than any CFL team could afford. It is rumoured the Bombers of the mid-thirties managed it for a little over $5,000.

When they arrived at the violinist's compartment door the midnight hour was rapidly approaching. Nevertheless, it seemed obvious (to them) that Kreisler would be only too glad to demonstrate his musical gifts for their talented teammate. They were wrong. The violinist wanted to sleep. No, he wouldn't provide even a brief rendition of his famous skills. And no, despite their pleading, he wouldn't even "practise a little."

"Gee," grumbled one of Hanson's disillusioned teammates, "how you do expect to become any damn good, Fritz, if you don't practise."

Oh, well. Even Fritz Hanson couldn't win them all.

Though Hanson was clearly their brightest star, he was far from their only talented import. Add Greg Kabat, Russ Rebholz, Bud Marquardt, Herb Peschel and playing-coach Bob Fritz to the list. There wasn't much wrong with a Canadian content that included Eddie James, Rosey Adelman, Lou Mogul, Arnie Coulter and Bill Cerretti, either. There are still old-timers around prepared to argue Dynamite Eddie James was the finest Canadian-born running back the team has ever had. Give or take his son, Gerry James (Little Dynamite), of course.

■ Cover of popular Tony Allan book, Grey Cup or Bust: *The first book on the Blue Bombers.*

To sign that group of players at today's prices would be far more than any CFL team could afford. It is rumoured the Bombers of the mid-thirties managed it for a little over $5,000.

As it turns out signing Hanson in a Fargo bar wasn't the only event of that era that picked an odd way to change the future of Canadian football. There was also the poker game played in the basement of an upscale home in River Heights. Most of the players were already members of the Bombers' board of directors, but on this occasion they invited a tall, gangly lawyer to take a seat in the game.

To the delight of his hosts the lawyer wound up the evening as the game's biggest loser. They were more impressed when he showed up the next day and paid off his losses in cash.

"They were so impressed, they asked me to become a member of the board the following year," G. Sydney Halter would confess years later.

"Sir Sydney," as he came to be known, never performed any spectacular feats on the playing field, but his achievements off it have proven equally important. He quickly proved his worth as

■ Sydney Halter, former Commissioner of the CFL: *Guided the league through Bomber glory days.*

a member of the Winnipeg executive. In 1956 the entire membership of a league now known as the CFL agreed with that assessment. They chose him to become their first commissioner. Today, many people would add the words "first and best," to that distinction.

Halter was a no-nonsense guy. He said what he meant and meant what he said. When the occasion demanded he spoke his mind in no uncertain terms. Even the interminable arguments over rules became far less intense during Halter's watch. Not many players, coaches or executive members chose to debate him for long.

The Depression be damned. Looking back over 75 years of Blue Bomber history, it's difficult to find an era where they found better building blocks to success than in the "Dirty 30s." They didn't make big money, of course. No one did. What they did gain was something that would prove infinitely more valuable—a reputation for providing consistently good entertainment. The predictable bonus was a new generation of talented Winnipeg athletes grew up with the goal of playing for the Blue Bombers.

As the team approached its 75th season in 2005 only two members of the old Thirties gang were still around to reminisce—fullback Bill Boivin and centre Mel Wilson. By then both had celebrated 90th birthdays. Boivin, a fullback in his playing days, didn't join the team until 1936. That left him out of the West's first Grey Cup win, but he was very much a part of the teams that collected Grey Cup rings for wins in 1939 and 1941.

In 1942 Boivin joined a much bigger team—the Canadian army. For the next four years his unit was Winnipeg Light Infantry. He returned to civilian life in 1945 with the rank of Captain, but he chose to remain a member of the WLI reserve unit where he soon rose to the rank of colonel. He also maintained a close association with the local sports scene.

When a hard-working young coach named Hal Mauthe approached him seeking financing for his junior basketball team Boivin agreed.

"But I told him my life would be a lot easier if his team always finished a fighting second," he confessed years later. "In amateur sport it costs a

■ Early CFL cards, circa 1950: *Learn the game and enjoy a hard piece of bubble gum.*

lot more money to finance a winner because it always involves inter-provincial travel."

For the next two seasons Boivin was forced to come up with an additional $1,500 to cover travel expenses for Mauthe's talented youngsters. They won back-to-back national junior hoop titles in '53 and '54.

"Nothing surprising about that," Mel would respond indignantly. "We linemen have always been more agile and lighter afoot than those Fancy Dan running backs and pass catchers. We had to learn to take quick, nifty little steps to keep from getting off balance and run over."

"I had to hit all my contacts at the Winnipeg Grain Exchange two years in a row," he remembers with a sly grin. "Well, why not? That's where the money was."

As things turned out Boivin's experience with his young basketball team would soon come in handy. Shortly after his team's travel expenses were paid, Bomber president Ralph Misener convinced him he was just the man to become general manager of the Blue Bombers in 1954. Boivin happily agreed.

During his first three years as GM Boivin's coach was Al Sherman. His record was good but it earned him no cigars. Those came later when he left Winnipeg to coach the New York Giants of the NFL. Maybe expanding his first name from Al to Allie made the difference. However, Boivin didn't do a bad job of replacing him. He hired Bud Grant.

Long after his retirement in Vancouver, Boivin recalls his sports career in Winnipeg with only one real regret. Somewhere along the way those Grey Cup rings he won in 1939 and 1941 had disappeared.

On his 90th birthday—as sharp as ever, though a little hard of hearing—he got them back. Family members and old friends had arranged to have exact replicas created as a gift.

"One of the best birthday presents I've ever had," Boivin added with a grateful grin.

Wilson, who played from 1937-1945, has no regrets at all. After nine seasons of fending off opposing tackles and linebackers, Wilson was able to retire with a singular distinction. To this day he remains the only centre ever to score a touchdown in a Grey Cup game. He didn't just recover a fumble in the enemy end zone, either. He scored on a designed play. He took a lateral from quarterback Bud Marquardt in the 1941 final and galloped the remaining five yards for the major score.

After his retirement Mel achieved considerable distinction in a competition most people would consider foreign territory for an old lineman. For several years following his retirement Mel and his partners won several ballroom dance competitions. When people suggested this seemed an unusual pursuit for a lineman who spent most of his playing days bent double and looking back through his legs to find his quarterback.

"Nothing surprising about that," Mel Wilson would respond indignantly. "We linemen have always been more agile and lighter afoot than those Fancy Dan running backs and pass catchers. We had to learn to take quick, nifty little steps to keep from getting off balance and run over."

THE WAR YEARS

From a football point of view, the decade of the Forties couldn't have had a much better start. Well, 1940 wasn't all that great but in 1941 with many of the players who won the brass ring in 1939 still around, The Blue Bombers captured the Cup for the third time in seven years. The bad news was that though they often played in the big game—seven times in all—they wouldn't win for another 17 years.

But before turning to the forties we need to reflect on the superb job Ryan did of finding talented players during those hungry thirties. Canada went to war in September 1939. It didn't end until May 1945. Even Ryan couldn't compete with the Canadian draft board. Like most Canadian institutions the Bombers suffered casualties. Jeff Nicklin went from superb running back to paratrooper. He was killed during the Normandy invasion. Today an award in his name is presented each year to the Western Conference's most outstanding player.

An interesting feature of the Ryan period is his claim that none of his players ever signed a contract. "We're an amateur team," he would slyly inform the newsmen of the time. "Besides, I'm a nice guy. People take my word."

Ryan would later move on to help create football dynasties in Montreal and Edmonton, but even half a century later it is not difficult to find evidence of his work. Larry Desjardins played only one season for the Bombers and by his own accounting not terribly well. Nevertheless, the $800 he was paid in 1942 put him through "embalming school" which prepared him to take over the family funeral service and, a few years later, the rough and tumble of provincial politics.

He was elected to the provincial legislature in the Ed Schreyer NDP government of the sixties. In fanciful mood Schreyer appointed him his minister of health. When a member of the opposition arose to inform the house their new health minister was a mortician Desjardins was ready with an answer. "Yes and you're a doctor," he replied. "I know because I've buried a lot of your mistakes."

The same approach that brought Hanson to the Bombers was equally effective in landing a 240-pound Minnesota lineman named Bert Oja. We are told George Halas, owner and coach of the NFL Chicago Bears, had offered the versatile lineman far more money than the Bombers could afford. Nevertheless, Winnipeg was able to present an offer Oja liked better. They paid him enough to cover his final year of dentistry at Minnesota. Then, when they learned he would need a degree from a Canadian school to practise in Manitoba, they enrolled him in the University of Alberta school of dentistry in 1936 and allowed him to commute to Winnipeg's football games. Dr. Bert Oja would become a prominent member of his post-football profession in Manitoba.

From 1942 to 1944 the Western Interprovincial Rugby Union ceased operations as Canada mounted a full-fledged war effort. Many football players joined the military but their football playing days weren't necessarily over. It was decided that civilian morale could be boosted by military sponsored football teams competing against one another. Thus began the Western

POST-WAR: A NEW ERA

BY BUD IRVING

The year 1945 saw a post-war reorganization of the Winnipeg Football Club. Bert Warwick was the coach, Bill Nairn his assistant. The team was made up of almost entirely Canadian players, a mixture of veteran players from a previous era and a number of players that were recruited from high school and junior and intermediate leagues. The old school consisted of Mel Wilson, Mo Simovich, Chester McCance, Lloyd Evenson, Wilf Daniels, Nate Shore, Norm Geller, Lloyd Boivin, Ken Draper, Rube Ludwig, Bert Iannone, Tiny Lucid, Kippie McFayden, Jack "Duke" Manners, Frank Mulvey and Danny Summers. The new hopefuls included Eddie Ogalski, Jimmy Foubister, Steve Bohunicki, Ron Gillies, Harold Bella, Elton Hobson, Harry Hood, Harry Johnston, Eddy Pollock, Kas Vidruk, Don Smith and yours truly, Bud Irving. Unquestionably the star of the team was McCance, who played every position on the team and also did the punting and placekicking.

We practised at Osborne Stadium and to the best of my knowledge not one of the players had a contract with the football club nor did any of them expect to be paid. At the end of the season, Tony Lucid advised me had just received a cheque for $350 from club president Arthur Chipman. My short walk to Chipman's office turned into a run and I ended up with $100 for the season. After a

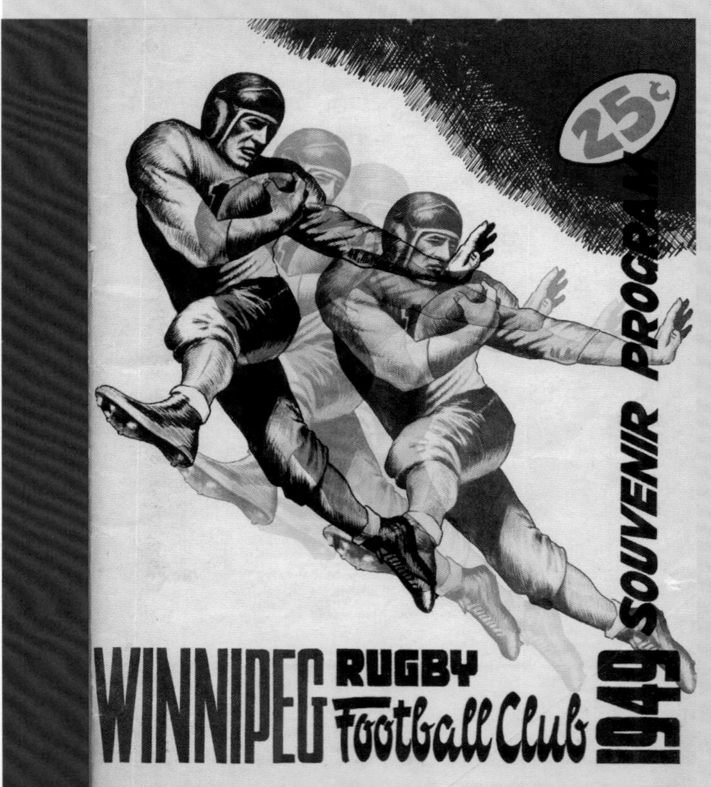

regular season that featured games against Minot State Teachers College, North Dakota State, North Dakota Fighting Sioux, Concordia College, Bemidji State Teachers College and Regina, we hosted the Western Final and beat Calgary 9-5 on a late touchdown by Lloyd Boivin. This nondescript group of non-imports lost the Grey Cup game to Joe Krol, Royal Copeland and the Toronto Argonauts 35-0, but I'll never forget the thrill each one of us experienced when we were standing on the 45-yard line listening to the national anthem prior to the start of the game. It's a cherished memory.

In 1946 the team hired a new coach named Jack West, who had been coaching at the University of North Dakota. West brought with him from Grand Forks Don Hiney, Walter Dobler and Bill Ordway while Martin Gainor and Bill Cerretti returned to the team. Lionel Wood, one of my high school buddies, also joined the team. Cerretti and Shore were considered our most ferocious players. Walt Dobler was the quarterback and Don Hiney was the only player that I had ever seen kick a field goal by drop-kicking the ball. The '46 season ended with the Bombers beating Calgary in a two game total point series and again losing the Grey Cup to the Argos in Toronto, 28-6.

Johnny Reagan, Bob Smith, Johnny Westrum and quarterback and punter Bob Sandberg joined our 1947 Blue Bomber team. For the third year in a row we defeated Calgary in the Western Final setting up yet another date at Varsity Stadium with the dreaded Argonauts. According to accounts of the game we used only 15 players and 9 of them played the full 60 minutes. By the final minute, we were exhausted. Coach West decided to gamble on a third down deep in our own end. Bert Iannone came up short of a first down on a guard-around play, we turned the ball over and Joe Krol kicked the winning single on the last play as the Argos prevailed 10-9.

1948 and '49 were miserable years. The Edmonton Eskimos rejoined the western conference in '48 and we were no match for a Calgary team that featured Keith Spaith and Woody Strode, among others. We finished with a 3-9 record. In '49 Frank (Butch) Larson, a two-time All-American end from the University of Minnesota, took over as head coach. He was aided by a leading junior coach in Winnipeg, Cam Doherty. A promising junior named George Depres was among the new faces that joined the team but we struggled to a 2-12 finish.

■ Blue Bomber guard, Bud Irving: *CFL All-Star in 1948.*

1950 was much better. Sol Kampf joined Butch Larson on the coaching staff, Canada Packers became the Bombers' new training field and there was an influx of American players led by Jack Jacobs from Okahoma via the Washington Redskins and Green Bay Packers. Jacobs was lured to Winnipeg with the promise that he would be able to play quarterback and he also proved to be one of the best defensive halfbacks Winnipeg had ever seen. Tom Casey and Buddy Tinsley were among the other import players to join the team. Tinsley was a tower of strength on an offensive line that included Glenn Johnson and John Brown. We went 10-4, defeated Edmonton in the Western Final, only to once again taste defeat in Toronto against the Argos, 13-0 in the famous Mud Bowl.

My six years with the Bombers, from 1945 to 1950, were looked upon as the years in which the Bombers were rejuvenated after the war and laid the foundation for the successful years that were to follow. In assembling these "memories" I gratefully acknowledge reference to Jim Foubister's scrapbook and the late Tony Allan's "Grey Cup or Bust."

Bud Irving played with the Bombers from 1945-1950.

Services Football League which lasted until 1944. In 1945, the Blue Bombers resumed operations and although there was no formal league that year, Winnipeg, Regina and Calgary formed teams to challenge for the Grey Cup. Winnipeg coach Bert Warwick led his team to a win over Calgary in the West final, but the Grey Cup game was no contest as Joe Krol and the Toronto Argos rolled to a 35-0 win over the Blue Bombers. In 1946, the Bombers lost the Grey Cup game again, this time 28-6 to the Argos. In 1947, star running back Bob Sandberg was brought in from Minnesota, giving the Bombers their best running attack since Fritz Hanson retired in 1945. But the season ended with another Grey Cup loss, this time 10-9 to the Argos as Krol booted the sinning single with no time left.

TRADING CLEATS FOR SCALPELS

There is, in fact, such a remarkable history of post-career success among the Bombers who played in the thirties and forties that it can't be dismissed as coincidence. Jim McPherson, a lineman who joined the Bombers in 1949 and Norm Hill, a tight end, both became doctors who went on to outstanding success. McPherson is today one of the leading practitioners at the famed Mayo Clinic in Rochester, Minnesota. Hill, began his football with the 1948 Stampeders (he caught the winning touchdown in the Grey Cup game) before returning to Winnipeg in 1950. Later he would become widely known as one of this country's leading neurosurgeons. He, too, would practice at the Mayo Clinic before returning to Winnipeg.

At one point Dr. Hill was called upon to remove a dangerous tumour from the brain of an old teammate, Moe Simovitch. Moe was never a star on the football field, but he went on to become one of the best known sports figures in the country as the "colour man" on Jack Wells' play-by-play football broadcasts.

Folklore claims Moe's final words before going under sedation were: "Don't fumble the ball you son of a bitch."

Was the rumour true?

"Actually, he said a lot worse than that," Hill recalls with a laugh.

That system put a lot of talented players, both Canadian and American, on the Winnipeg roster, but what seems even more impressive is how many of them went on to greater success when their playing days were over. It is difficult to believe the discipline forced on them by jobs and further education didn't play a significant role.

Sam Fabro spent only a single season (1942) with the Bombers and a lot of that on the bench, but he went on to become president of a large national carpet company. It's hard to find a charitable organization Sam hasn't helped over the last half century.

Besides playing a mean game in the Bombers' offensive line from 1945-1950 H.K. (Bud) Irving went on to become a highly successful lawyer. In fact, he became so engrossed in meting out justice he became a tough as nails CFL official for a number of years.

George Depres and Paul Cholakis were so successful at St. Paul's college towards the end of the forties they became known as the "Touchdown Twins." Depres threw the passes. Cholakis caught and ran them in for touchdowns. They had planned to accept an invitation to play for the B.C. Lions in 1949. That ended when Cholakis' dad informed him his services were more needed in the family flower business. They joined the Bombers for the '49 season, but by then Coach Frank Larson had made other plans.

No matter. Depres went on to serve 15 years as general manager of Winnipeg Enterprises, the volunteer group that used to operate the stadium where the Bombers play their home games. More than once Depres came to their rescue when they were scrambling to meet increasing salary demands from their players. Meanwhile, Paul Cholakis has seen the family flower business flourish.

Bill Orban is another ex-Bomber who had a short career, but a memorable post-football career. He broke his leg in the first and only game he ever played. The injury probably had something to do with the exercise program he subsequently devised. Actually, it was two programs—one called 5BX and 10BX. Both programs were eagerly accepted by the

Archives of Manitoba

■ Blue Bomber running back Ed Bilski, 1948: *Will someone please hurry up and invent the face-mask?*

Royal Canadian Air Force. In fact, Bud Grant borrowed liberally from both systems during his 10-year term as Winnipeg's head coach.

Ironically, one of the great stories involving a player from the forties didn't unfold until well into 1958. The late Don Smith, a tough, straight-ahead fullback in his playing days, took the lead in organizing a fund-raising dinner for the 1957 Blue Bombers who had lost the Grey Cup to the Hamilton Tiger-Cats a few weeks earlier. By then a city alderman and successful insurance broker, Smitty booked the biggest dining room in Winnipeg. The food was good, the drink was plentiful, the after-dinner speakers properly amusing.

He had even persuaded the victorious Ticats to lend him the Grey Cup for the occasion. Like most people at the dinner Smith had consumed his fair share of liquor. However, he didn't forget his promise to put the Grey Cup in the box it came in and ship it back to Hamilton. His intentions were above reproach, but somehow he managed to trip on his way back to his car conveniently parked in the lane behind the hotel.

Unhappily the cup flew from its box and broke in two when it hit the pavement. Even worse, the cup part had rolled under a loading dock and disappeared. He was on his hands and knees under the loading dock when the police car happened to drive up.

"What are you doing down there," the cop demanded.

"I'm looking for the Grey Cup," Smitty answered truthfully.

"Sure you are," replied the doubtful lawman.

It was only after he crawled out from under the dock, proudly brandishing the cup—or what was left of it—did the officer shake his head, climb back in his car and leave.

The next day Smitty had the cup expertly repaired and on its way back to Hamilton. With no one the wiser—until now. ■

■ Indian Jack Jacobs: *Talent, intensity, heart and a big-time throwing arm.*

CHAPTER 2

Winnipeg Tribune, University of Manitoba Archives

1950-1969

BECOMING A POWERHOUSE

BY BOB PICKEN

He broke the huddle with a clap of his hands, and sized up the opposition alignment as his teammates fanned out into the spread formation. His demeanor was confident and purposeful. His lips curled into a scowl, and then he barked his signals. He took the snap, pumped once, and fired his pass with deadly accuracy.

This was the quarterback who changed the complexion of Canadian football forever. This was the player who electrified football crowds across the West, and lifted the game to a new level. This was the man with the golden arm who had the sole intention of hitting his passing targets, and winning with an aerial bombardment.

This was Indian Jack Jacobs, and he was something special.

Archives of Manitoba

■ (From left) Equipment manager Bob Jones, Jack Jacobs, George Trafton, Dick Huffman: *On the sidelines at Osborne Stadium, circa 1952.*

SHORT YARDAGE

Did you know: All-star Tom Casey ingratiated himself with Winnipeggers by volunteering during the 1950 flood within a few days of his arriving in the city.

Jacobs was a proud, full-blooded Cherokee who starred in his college days at Oklahoma, and believed his ability as a quarterback was never appreciated in eight years in the National Football League with Cleveland, Washington and Green Bay from 1942 to 1949.

For that reason, and the $6,000 per year he was offered, Jacobs was receptive to the approach from Blue Bombers president Ralph Misener in 1950. Misener had been tipped about Jacobs' disenchantment in Green Bay, and after checking his background, invited him to Winnipeg.

Jacobs signed his first Bomber contract on Misener's dining room table, after insisting in the terms that he would be the team's quarterback, and would not be switched to a defensive halfback position.

Signing Jacobs was the first item on the agenda for Misener, who was determined to snap the Bombers out of the doldrums of two losing seasons, 3-9 in 1948 and 2-12 in '49. It was obvious the quality of imports had to be upgraded. Calgary Stampeders ran roughshod over western teams for two seasons, led by ex-NFLers Keith Spaith, Woody Strode and Sugarfoot Anderson. The Stamps were an unbeaten 12-0 in 1948, and compiled a 22-game winning streak on the way to 13-1 the next year.

Teams were allowed seven imports in 1950, and Misener set a $70,000 player budget and went shopping. He needed a key receiver to go with Jacobs, and found one in Tom Casey, who had played with New York Yankees in the All-American Conference, and with Hamilton Wildcats of the Ontario Rugby Football Union in 1949. Casey wanted to enter a medical school, and he was accepted at the University of Manitoba. The fact he also turned out to be an excellent running back,

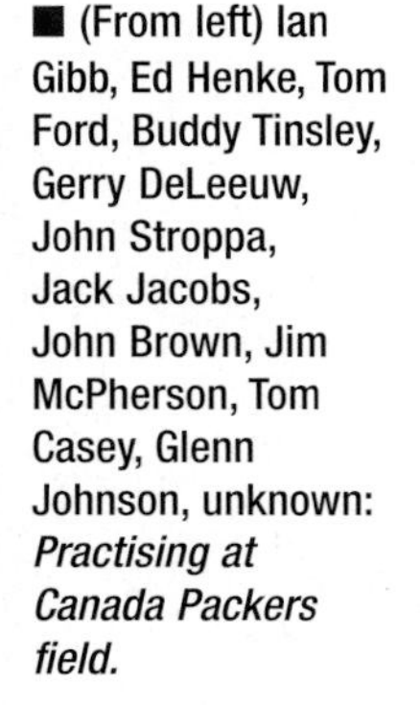

■ (From left) Ian Gibb, Ed Henke, Tom Ford, Buddy Tinsley, Gerry DeLeeuw, John Stroppa, Jack Jacobs, John Brown, Jim McPherson, Tom Casey, Glenn Johnson, unknown: *Practising at Canada Packers field.*

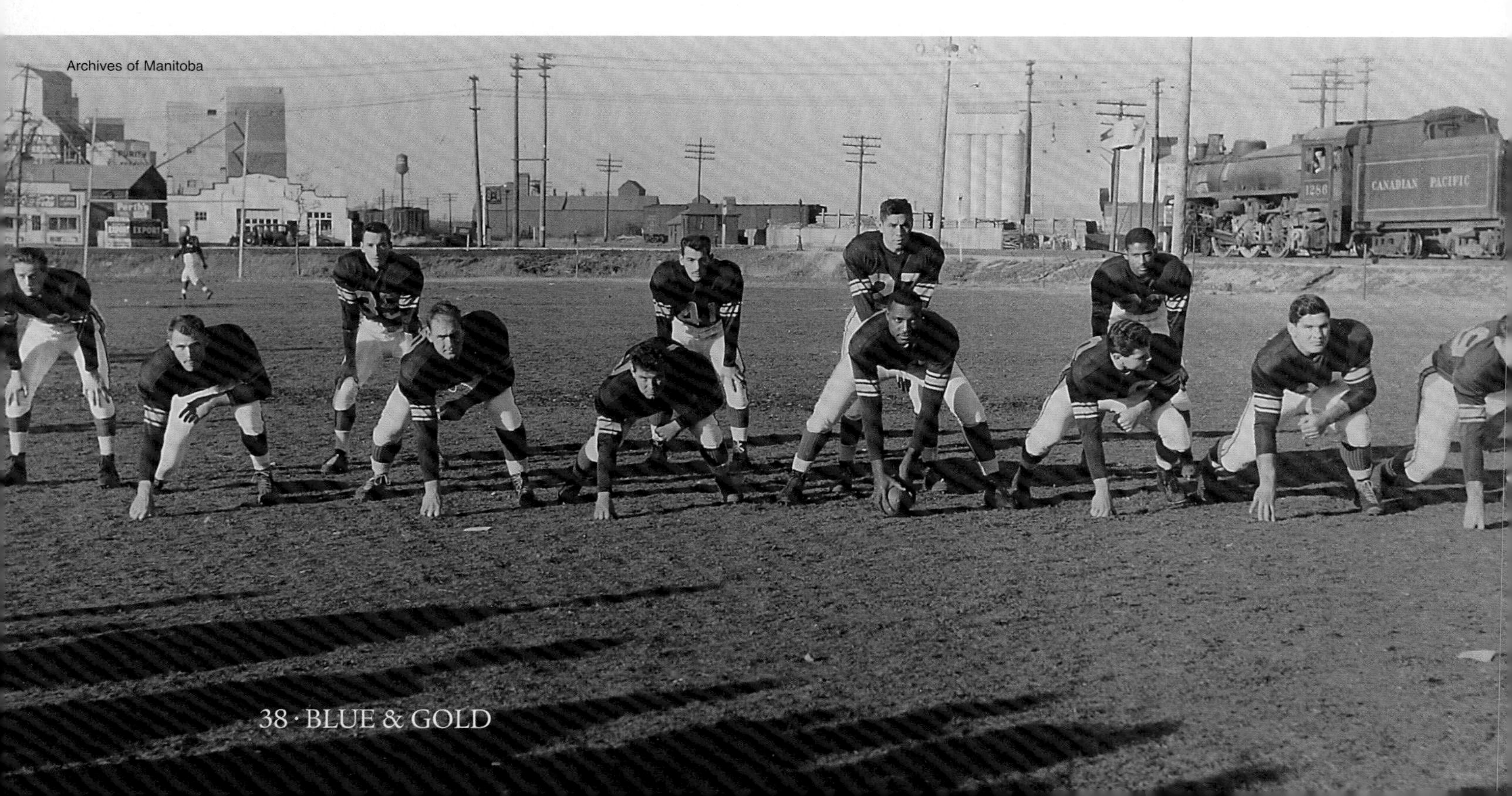

Archives of Manitoba

■ **Big Buddy Tinsley being helped off the field:**
A rare injury for the seven-time all-star.

Western Canada Pictorial Index

VICKI CZARNECKI: THE RIGHT HAND GIRL

BY BOB PICKEN

She called herself a "quiet, very shy farm girl" from Roblin, Manitoba, who somehow became the cog in the Blue Bomber administrative machinery for 37 years. So significant were her contributions she became the first woman elected to the Bomber Hall of Fame.

■ 'Miss Vicki': *Long time bookkeeper, chief cook and bottle washer.*

Vicki Czarnecki was a secretary, accountant, and general assistant to Bomber general managers from 1954 to 1991. She was hired by Bill Boivin, and after four years under his tutelage, she served under Jim Ausley, Bud Grant, Terry Hind, Earl Lunsford, Paul Robson, and Cal Murphy.

Over the course of those years, she handled the bulk of the paper work for the Bombers, did the payroll, accounts payable, handled expense accounts, processed player contracts, and helped her GMs balance the books.

Now living comfortably in retirement, Czarnecki said, "It was a lot of work, but also a lot of fun. I have no regrets. I dealt with some great people, team officials and volunteers. Yes, we had a few player prima donnas, but there also were some high class athletes who wore Bomber uniforms."

Czarnecki saw the club operation grow and expand over the years. It developed from basic football functions to extensive involvement in major business promotions. She was in the Bomber office for the winning seasons under Grant, and all the frustration of the losing campaigns until the Bombers won Grey Cups in 1984, 1988 and '90.

She has some fond memories of Grant, who coached the team in its glory years, and served as its general manager from 1964-66. "It often was said that Bud was cold and withdrawn," she said. "But he really could be a practical joker. I came into my office one day and found a big envelope on my desk. When I opened it there was a dead mouse in it!"

Czarnecki still is a football fan, and wouldn't pass on a Bomber game. "I'm a season ticket holder," she revealed. "And I want to be there when they start to be a winner again."

Bob Picken is a veteran CBC sports broadcaster.

and a first-class citizen was to make him a Bomber legend in his seven years in blue-and-gold.

Next came Buddy Tinsley, an affable Texan who had been a two-way tackle at Baylor University and with Los Angeles Dons of the AAC. Buddy and his wife Hazel grew up in a small town, 35 miles from Houston. Neither one of them liked the big city life in Los Angeles, and when the AAC merged with the NFL in 1950, Tinsley thought it was time to look elsewhere.

Agreeing to play both ways in Winnipeg, Tinsley received a larger contract than Jacobs, \$6,500, plus a \$1,000 signing bonus. He proved to be worth every penny, and became an inspirational team player for 11 seasons with the Bombers, earning seven all-star selections.

Winnipeg Free Press

Jacobs was influential in luring tackle Glenn Johnson and split end Bill Kelley, former teammates at Green Bay, to the Bombers, and Tinsley recommended huge centre John Brown, a 6-foot-five 250-pounder, who also was available after the folding of Los Angeles Dons. The seventh import acquired was defensive end Ed Henke, who bolted from San Francisco 49ers.

Misener and coach Frank Larson also recruited in the Canadian ranks. Four newcomers came in from Ontario—halfback Tommy Ford, who was moving here to coach swimming, receiver Sleepy Knowles, fullback Andy Sokol, and halfback George McPhail, a Winnipeg native who had played in Ottawa and Regina.

Those additions produced the nucleus of talent that reversed the Bomber fortunes. More important, the style of play they produced lifted the game from a senior, semi-pro category toward full-blown professionalism that soon began to fill the stadiums across the country.

■ (Foreground) The legendary Jack Jacobs and Winnipeg Stadium: *'The house that Jack built'.*

JACK JACOBS HELPED TURN BIG BLUE INTO A PRO FRANCHISE

Jacobs was dynamic. When he wasn't threading the needle on passes to Casey, Kelley, or local product Bud Korchak—who played the old flying wing position—he was lofting towering punts toward the fences in Osborne Stadium, with its below-regulation 100-yard field

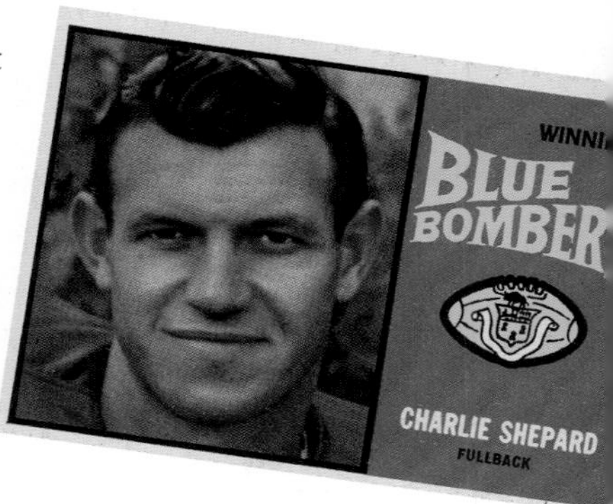

■ **Running back and punter, Charlie Shepard:** ***Set the record for the longest punt in Blue Bomber history—95 yards—in 1960.***

Archives of Manitoba

■ **Sylvia Sveinson, Blue Bomber Queen, 1953:** ***Great throwing motion.***

Winnipeg Free Press

and 10-yard end zones. The Bombers won six out of seven home games in 1950, and the roar of capacity crowds shook the foundation of the adjacent Amphitheatre and rattled the Golden Boy atop the legislature across the street.

Casey once declared that Jacobs brought out the best in an athlete. "You had to go all out when Jake was the quarterback," he said. "He had no patience with players who were not concentrating, or lacked motivation. He had an intense passion for the game, and his passing ability was remarkable."

Jacobs guided the Bombers to first place and an overall 10-4 record in 1950, in what then was known as the Western Interprovincial Football Union. They lost a 17-16 cliffhanger to the Edmonton Eskimos in the opener of a best-of-three western final, but the Bombers rebounded to win two straight and the series. In game three, Jacobs punted for nearly a 50-yard average, and repeatedly backed the Eskimos into poor field position. He also scored two touchdowns on quarterback keepers in a 29-6 victory.

The Bombers advanced to the Grey Cup final in Toronto, and what turned out to be one of the team's all time major disappointments. Clearly, after their terrific western season, the Bombers were expected to challenge the Argonauts, a longtime nemesis, with superior talent and definite momentum going for them after beating Edmonton.

The Bomber performance was shockingly miserable, and was blamed on field conditions at Varsity Stadium. Toronto was hit by a heavy snowfall a few days before the game, and in trying to clear the field groundskeepers used a bulldozer and ripped the surface into a sea of gooey, slippery mud–the game thus was baptized as "the Mud Bowl."

The Argos made adjustments that provided an edge. They applied the longest cleats allowed to aid their footing, and quarterback Al Dekdebrun taped thumbtacks to his fingers to help in gripping the ball. In contrast, the Bombers were skidding and sliding all over the field, and Jacobs had the worst game of his career with only two completions in 11 pass attempts.

Jacobs guided the Bombers to first place and an overall 10-4 record in 1950, in what then was known as the Western Interprovincial Football Union.

Jacobs fumbled twice, and Toronto capitalized on the turnovers for two field goals. He also had a punt blocked, the Argos recovered, and drove in for the game's only touchdown by Dekdebrun. It was a 13-0 debacle in favour of Toronto, and the Bomber ineptitude led to the firing of coach Larson.

One other incident became part of "Mud Bowl" mythology, because Buddy Tinsley disclaimed its authenticity. After solid contact, he was lying prone in a puddle of mud and water, and referee Hec Crighton reportedly thought that Tinsley was about to drown, and rolled him onto

LEO LEWIS: THE LINCOLN LOCOMOTIVE

BY BOB IRVING

Bud Grant called him "the greatest football player I ever coached." Grant was referring to his time coaching with both the Winnipeg Blue Bombers and the NFL's Minnesota Vikings when he paid running back Leo Lewis that ultimate compliment.

Leo Lewis came to the Blue Bombers in 1955 from Lincoln University in Missouri. It didn't take long for the Bombers to realize they had landed a very special player in the "Lincoln Locomotive." Lewis wore jersey #99 during his rookie season, then switched to #29 in 1956, and for the next 10 years, defensive players in the CFL were mesmerized by the soft-spoken product of Columbia, Missouri. Teammate Ron Latourelle says Lewis was a phenomenal athlete. "His body could go in several directions at one time and he had unbelievable vision." Latourelle says offensive linemen Ed Kotowich and Cornel Piper ran for miles in practice so they could lead Lewis downfield on his famous sweeps. Latourelle says, "it was beautiful to watch all three of them moving around the end and downfield." Latourelle adds that few players had more character than Lewis. "He was quiet, humble but a tremendous leader who led by example."

Lewis still holds the Bombers all-time record for yards rushing, 8,861. His 6.6 yard rushing average is the best in CFL history among running backs. Lewis also set a club record that still stands for receiving yards by a running back of 4,251. He is fifth on the CFL's all-time list for combined yards with 18,576. And his spectacular career kickoff return average of 29.1 yards is second only in league history to the 35.2 yards posted by Edmonton's Larry Highbaugh.

Winnipeg Free Press

■ Leo Lewis: *Four Grey Cup championships and a member of the CFL Hall-of-Fame.*

■ (Below) The Lewis family: *Leo Lewis Day at Winnipeg Stadium, 1966.*

Western Canada Pictorial Index

Lewis lists Hamilton's Angelo Mosca as his toughest opponent. He says Jackie Parker is the greatest player he ever saw in the CFL. And he particularly admired Bud Grant's coaching style, saying, "he was not a curser or a loud talker, but he had a way of soft talking you into doing his will."

Leo Lewis looks back fondly on his 11 years with the Blue Bombers. "Those years in Winnipeg were years of happiness and joy. The citizens treated me with respect and kindness and I will never forget it. Even though that was many years ago, the recollection of that period of time is always filled with tender, warm memories." Bomber fans would no doubt return the compliment to the classy Lewis, the "greatest football player" Bud Grant ever coached.

Bob Irving is sports director of CJOB 68 Radio.

■ The best fans in the country: *Of course, alcohol has no bearing on the enthusiasm of the Bomber faithful.*

his back. Buddy called it "hogwash," or maybe more appropriately "mudwash."

The chastened Bombers vowed to make amends, but it took three seasons before they earned a chance. Meanwhile, team management pinned the goathorns on Larson, and replaced him with firebrand George Trafton, who brought a highly volatile dimension to the coaching position.

Trafton was a guttural, profane, explosive loudmouth, but his playing and coaching credentials in the NFL were impeccable. During 12 seasons at centre for the Chicago Bears, he liked to be known as the "toughest man in football." He came to Winnipeg from an assistant coaching position with Los Angeles Rams, and recommended another disgruntled player to the Bombers.

Jacobs signed his first Bomber contract on Misener's dining room table, after insisting in the terms that he would be the team's quarterback, and would not be switched to a defensive halfback position.

Dick Huffman was a truly brilliant lineman, one of the best ever to grace a Winnipeg gridiron, but to get him in 1951 the Bombers had to fight a legal battle against a Los Angeles injunction. Receiver Neil Armstrong also wanted to bolt from Philadelphia Eagles, and the necessary loophole was found in the option clause of NFL contracts to acquire them.

Their presence failed to ignite the team, but Trafton recognized the need to inject promising Canadian talent, and he welcomed two outstanding homebrews in running back Lorne "Boom Boom" Benson and defensive end Tommy Lumsden. Win or lose, the Bombers continued to play to capacity crowds, and justified the planning of a new stadium.

The Bombers, Edmonton and Saskatchewan finished in a three-way tie with 8-6 records in '51, and the Roughriders, led by Glen Dobbs who rivalled Jacobs for his passing and kicking ability, earned the first place bye on a best for-and-against scoring record.

The sudden death semi-final was another bitter pill to swallow. Edmonton beat the Bombers in a defensive struggle 4-1, and this time the result couldn't be attributed to the playing conditions. Saskatchewan topped Edmonton in a three-game western final, but lost the Grey Cup game to Ottawa 21-14.

■ CFL referee Paul Dojack and Bomber head coach Al Sherman, 1956: *'And another thing, you're calling a great game, great I tell you'.*

ADDING CANADIANS TO THE MIX

The next two seasons had enigmatic parallels. The Bombers dominated the regular season with a 12-3-1 record in 1952, but lost the best-of-three western final to Edmonton after winning the first game. Then the Eskimos

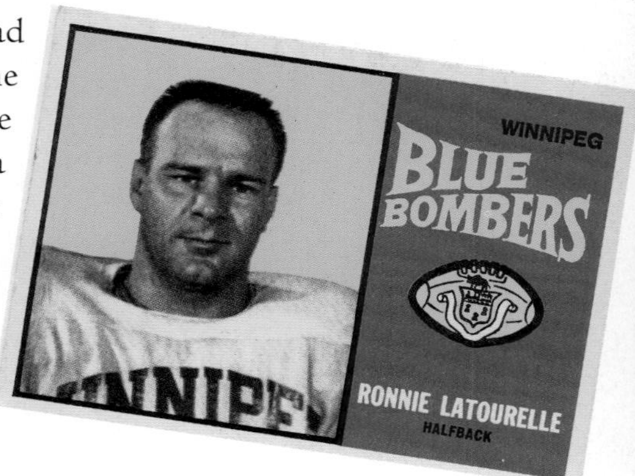

GORDIE MACKIE: TRAINER TO THE STARS

BY BOB PICKEN

It now is a full fledged profession called Athletic Therapy, but back in the days when Gordie Mackie started, the cuts, bumps, and bruises were treated by people simply known as "trainers."

Their work has become a major supporting force in professional and amateur sports over the years, and Mackie was at the centre of the development in Manitoba for nearly 40 years.

He has seen an enormous assortment of injuries in a multitude of sports, and treated many exceptional athletes on assignment to the Olympic Games, the Pan American Games, the World Aquatic Championships, and the World University Games.

Born in Winnipeg, Mackie served in the navy in World War Two, and became interested in the training aspects of sport at the Montreal YMCA after his discharge. He completed a physiotherapy course through the Department of Veterans Affairs after returning to Winnipeg to operate the Madison Boxing Club.

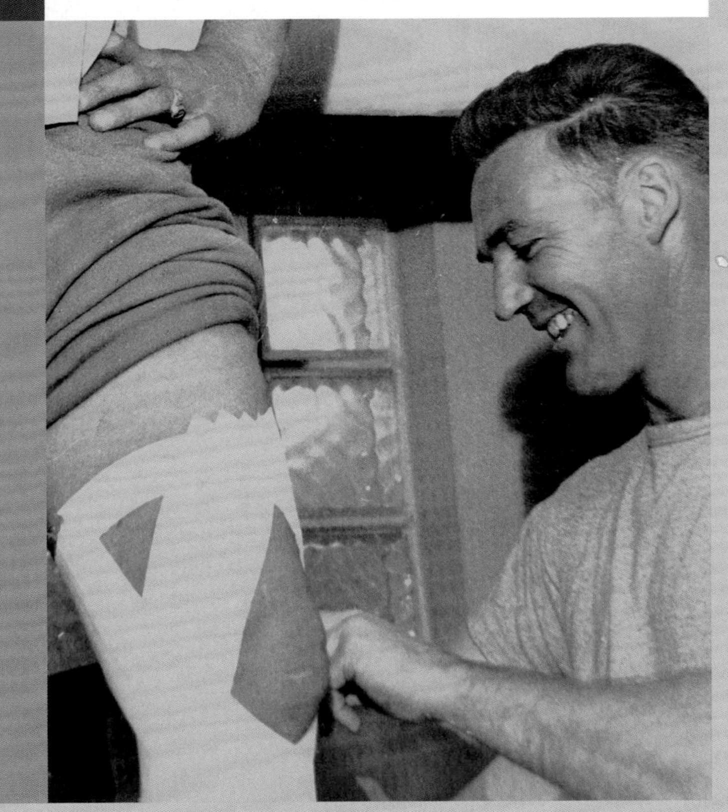

■ Trainer Gord Mackie taping up a knee: *Loved by all and a man the players could trust.*

Hugh Allen Photography

In 1953, Gordie became an assistant therapist at the West Point Military Academy, working with athletes in football, soccer, track and field, and boxing. He was on the sidelines in Philadelphia for the Army-Navy football games for two years.

"The two years I spent at West Point were a tremendous experience for me," he said. "It was like taking post-graduate studies in therapy, and I still recall having shivers from the super-charged atmosphere at the Army-Navy football games."

He spent the 1955-59 period as therapist for baseball's original Winnipeg Goldeyes in the summer, and for the Winnipeg Warriors and St. Paul Saints professional hockey teams in the winter seasons.

In 1959, Blue Bomber general manager Jim Ausley came calling. "He hired me as the team's therapist, and I wound up spending the next 11 seasons with the football club," he recalled. "I believe we improved the training methods during that time frame, and the Bombers always were receptive to our requests to upgrade the equipment."

Mackie moved to the University of Manitoba in 1970, and created a physical therapy program. He taught his craft as part of the physical education curriculum at the university, and operated a therapy clinic on campus for 17 years.

Mackie now lives contentedly in Charleswood, and still works half days tending to the aches and pains of "close friends and old codgers." In the football season, Mackie rubs shoulders regularly in the east side alumni lounge with the team's old guard.

Gordie Mackie's service to sport in Manitoba was recognized in 1987, when he was inducted as a builder into the provincial Sports Hall of Fame.

Bob Picken is a veteran CBC sports reporter.

surged to the top in '53 with a 12-4 record, won the opener of the final, but dropped the next two and the third place Bombers went to the Grey Cup.

Trafton added another non-import star-to-be in '52. Gerry James vaulted from the high school campus at Kelvin to launch a 12-year-career as a Bomber running back. Korchak became the team's placement kicker when Joe "the Toe" Aguirre departed, and his prowess earned the Winnipeg north end product western all-star honors for two campaigns. On the import scene, Joe "Black Magic" Zaleski, a deft ball handler, offered a change-of-pace as a back-up quarterback to Jacobs.

In 1953, a player arrived in Winnipeg who was one of Minnesota's greatest athletes, and over the course of 14 seasons as a player and coach Harry Peter "Bud" Grant was a key figure in the most successful era in Blue Bomber history.

TACKLE / WINNIPEG BLUE BOMBERS
ROGER SAVOIE

(From left) Buddy Leake, Bud(dy) Grant, Buddy Alliston, Buddy Tinsley, 1956: *Hey Buddy, can you spare a dime?*

Winnipeg Free Press

University of Manitoba Archives

■ Defensive end Herb Gray, 1958: *Seven-time All-Star and four Grey Cup championships.*

In that '53 season, Grant, Armstrong, and Casey provided Jacobs with a brilliant receiving corps for the first year at Winnipeg Stadium, often called "The House That Jack Built," but the team was a lacklustre 8-8 on the regular season.

Benson lit a spark in the opener of a two-game total-point semi-final. The rugged Daniel McIntyre-Weston Wildcat graduate blasted his way to a record six touchdowns in leading the Bombers to a 43-5 trouncing of the Roughriders in Regina. Benson's achievement doesn't show in the Bomber record book because it came in the playoffs, and it was matched in 1956 by a super running back from Minnesota, Bob McNamara.

After advancing to the final, the Bombers were clobbered 25-7 by the Eskimos at Clarke Stadium

Surprise, surprise. Trafton inserted Zaleski to replace Jacobs, and he guided the Bombers to a 21-17 equalizing victory before a then record crowd of 17,434 at the new stadium.

in Edmonton to open the best-of-three series. The teams travelled to Winnipeg for game two, and there was little optimism in the Bomber camp.

Surprise, surprise. Trafton inserted Zaleski to replace Jacobs, and he guided the Bombers to a 21-17 equalizing victory before a then record crowd of 17,434 at the new stadium. Back they went to Edmonton for the wrap-up, and the game had a story-book ending for the Bombers.

After the league's initial Schenley award winner Billy Vessels put the Eskimos up 12-6 in the third quarter, Jacobs replaced Zaleski who had started at quarterback. He was intercepted, and the Eskimos scored again for an 18-6 lead (touchdown points were five plus the convert at that time) going into the fourth quarter.

Jacobs passed to Len Meltzer for a touchdown, Edmonton charged right back and a Normie Kwong major made it 24-12. Then came some

■ Foreground from left: Quarterbacks Kenny Ploen, Eagle Day, Gino Cappilletto, Jim Van Pelt.

■ Two-way Kenny Ploen, turning the corner in the 1958 Grey Cup game: *One of the greatest Grey Cup games in history.*

A DARK SATURDAY: NOVEMBER 19, 1960

BY ROGER CURRIE

■ Ken Ploen and wife Janet, 1960:
Behind every great man…

Western Canada Pictorial Index

Adolescent males tend to live and die with their sports heroes, and for me those heroes were the Winnipeg Blue Bombers. I turned ten just as the Bombers' greatest Golden Age began. It was 1957, when Bud Grant took over the coaching reins, and the pride of Iowa, Kenny Ploen made his debut at quarterback. For five of the next six seasons, Winnipeg was the western representative in the Grey Cup and they ended up winning four of them. That remarkable run was interrupted in 1960, when they broke my 13-year-old heart.

After losing to Hamilton in the 1957 Grey Cup, the Bombers had won the championship in impressive fashion the next two years. If anything, the 1960 Blue Bombers were even stronger. They began the season with ten straight victories, a team record that stood for more than 40 years. After giving way to Jim Van Pelt for a while, Kenny Ploen was once again the number one quarterback and we were in good hands. But it was a hand injury that proved crucial in 1960 as the Bombers defended their western conference title against the dreaded Edmonton Eskimos, led by Jackie Parker.

In those days the western final was a best of three affair. The Bombers won the first game 22-16 at Edmonton's Clarke Stadium, but in the process Kenny Ploen broke a small bone in his throwing hand. For the second game two days later in Winnipeg, Bud Grant handed the ball to backup quarterback Vernon Cole. Edmonton won the game 10-5, setting up the deciding match on Saturday, November 19th. Grant didn't announce his starting quarterback prior to the game, and a huge roar went up when Ploen trotted onto the field with his right hand heavily bandaged.

Both teams were crippled by injuries. Bill Smith, who later served as one of Edmonton's most popular mayors, played defensive back for the Eskimos with a cast on his arm. It wasn't classic football, but it was typical of the western playoffs in those years. The Bombers clung to a 2-1 (yes, that's correct) lead with just over a minute to go in the game.

Scrimmaging on their own 30 yard line, a first down would enable them to run out the clock. Kenny Ploen ran the ball to the left. He made enough for the first down but fumbled it away when tackled. Two plays later, Edmonton's Tommy Joe Coffey lined up to try a field goal. He had missed four in a row, and surely he would miss again. I covered my eyes, thinking that might help. I heard the roar of the crowd...and the rest was silence. Coffey made the field goal, and the Eskimos won the game 4-2. For quite a few hours afterwards I did not speak. I could not speak. I didn't cry, but I was inconsolable.

In retrospect, someone should have been reading something like Ernest Thayer's famous poem 'Casey at the Bat'. The trauma of that dark Saturday did not completely heal until the following season when Winnipeg won the Grey Cup in overtime thanks to a touchdown run by Kenny Ploen. By then I was 14, and life was good.

■ Farrell Funston: *Fell on the ball in the West final to send Winnipeg to the 1965 Grey Cup game.*

Winnipeg Free Press

vintage Jacobs passing. He hit Bud Grant on a 60-yard touchdown bomb, and connected to Keith Pearce for another from 38 yards out to tie the score at 24-all.

Edmonton responded by marching back to the Bomber 21-yard-line with less than two minutes to go. Eskimo quarterback Claude Arnold then made a fateful mistake. Instead of setting up a winning field goal or single, he chose to pass toward Rollie Miles.

Bomber defensive back Dave Skrein intercepted it on the Winnipeg 15-yard-line, and took off for the Edmonton goalline. At the Bomber 45, he noticed the fleet-footed Casey running beside him, and Skrein threw a lateral pass. Casey caught it, zoomed into the Eskimo end zone, and the Bombers had scored a remarkable 30-24 victory.

One more hurdle was needed to reach the Grey Cup final. The Bombers had to play a semi-final against ORFU champion Toronto Balmy Beach, and on a wintery day at Winnipeg Stadium, they won it 24-4.

Hamilton Tiger-Cats supplied the '53 Grey Cup opposition, in the first of many confrontations between the teams in the title game over the years. Like 1950, the Bombers seemed to be primed and ready to scale the heights, but once again they couldn't get the job done.

Jacobs put up tremendous passing numbers this time at Varsity Stadium, 28 completions in 48 attempts for 326 yards, but outside of a one-yard plunge for a touchdown by Gerry James in the third quarter, the Bombers fizzled in the red zone.

They trailed 12-6 late in the fourth quarter and made one last spirited drive that covered 103 yards. With time for one more play at the Hamilton three-yard-line, hoping for a tie and overtime, Jacobs passed to Casey near the goalline.

As he reached for the reception, Casey was belted by Hamilton defensive back Lou Kusserow, and the ball popped loose and hit the turf. It was ruled an incompletion, and though the Bombers argued for interference, game films showed Kusserow's hit came after Casey touched the ball, and he was short of the end zone anyway.

Kusserow was credited with precise anticipation. "I knew that Jacobs would pass, and he'd try for Casey. Tom was Jake's go-to guy when he needed a big play all season," he recalled. "I wasn't expecting anything else."

That was to be the last chance for Jacobs to reach the pinnacle in Canadian football, and it also spelled the end for Trafton in Winnipeg. His contract wasn't renewed, and he was replaced in 1954 by Al Sherman, an excellent tactical coach who had served under Steve Owen for five years as the backfield coach of the New York Giants.

■ Culver Riley: *President, Winnipeg Football Club—1952.*

■ Dick Huffman: *Proving that linemen sometime have muscle to go along with fat.*

Manitoba Sports Hall of Fame

SHORT YARDAGE

Did you know: In 1960 and with the game out of reach, the ball was handed off up the middle to popular running back Gerry James while the line allowed Saskatchewan linebacker Ron Acheson to go unblocked. Gerry bit the dust and the entire offence was in stitches.

Jacobs and Trafton had been at loggerheads during most of the coach's three seasons in Winnipeg, differing over play calls and the offensive system. Jacobs had a better working relationship with Sherman, but often was befuddled by the new coach's "revolving door manoeuvres" with his running backs. After the '54 season, in which the Bombers finished third and lost to Edmonton in the Western final, Jacobs retired.

Sherman was not on the same page as Trafton in another respect. He preferred imports to Canadians at key positions, and offered minimal encouragement to local players. The Bombers had records of 8-6-2, 7-9, and 9-7 in Sherman's three seasons, but weren't in a class with the Eskimo juggernauts that won three straight Grey Cup crowns.

■ (from left) Bud Grant, Joe Zaleski, John Michels: *The brains behind four Grey Cup wins.*

Winnipeg Free Press

THE GOLDEN YEARS

After the 1956 season, Bomber president Jim Russell and general manager Bill Boivin fired Sherman, and made an inspirational move that truly altered the team's destiny. Russell saw exceptional leadership potential in Bud Grant, and offered him the position of player-coach. The 29-year-old Grant, with no coaching experience, was ready to accept the challenge, but quickly decided to hang up his cleats as a player.

It was the dawn of the "golden years" of Bomber football. In 10 seasons at the helm, the "Silver Fox" guided the team to 102 regular season wins, a 20-10-1 post season record, five western titles and four Grey Cups. His strong suit was player evaluation skill, and like Trafton, he realized the quality of Canadian talent would determine success or the lack of it.

Grant and his first assistant coach Wayne Robinson nurtured local players like Steve Patrick, Roger Savoie, and Cec Luining in the defensive line, former Montreal soccer star Gord Rowland at linebacker, plus the versatile Nick Miller, Norm Rauhaus, Ron "Pepe" Latourelle, and Henry Janzen in the defensive backfield.

He moulded his championship offence around more non-imports, centre George Druxman, outstanding running guards Ed Kotowich and Cornel Piper, and durable running back Gerry James.

To be sure, Grant also had superlative Americans to spearhead his winning teams. Front and centre in that respect was Kenny Ploen, often termed an on-field extension of Grant for savvy and field generalship, the brilliant running back Leo Lewis, fullback-punter Charlie Shepard, defensive end Herbie Gray, linemen Frank Rigney,

■ Running back Bob McNamara: *Scored a CFL record six touchdowns against the B.C. Lions on October 13, 1956.*

Dave Burkholder, Gar Warren, and Jack Delveaux, and wide receivers Ernie Pitts and Farrell Funston.

Coaching was brilliant too. Robinson was here for the 1957 and '58 seasons, Joe Zaleski joined the group in '58, and Johnny Michels succeeded Robinson in 1959. Grant, Zaleski, and Michels formed a unique trio; Grant, always stoic, cool and observant; Zaleski, the instructive guiding hand who was closest to the players; and Michels, firm and demanding, a motivator who built team confidence.

Ploen came to Winnipeg as a 1957 Rose Bowl hero for Iowa, recruited by Grant to run the same

Winnipeg Tribune, University of Manitoba Archives

■ Leo Lewis in the 1962 Grey Cup, aka the 'Fog Bowl': *Catch me if you can.*

winged-T offence he learned under Forrest Evashevski, the coach of the Hawkeyes. The Bomber running game developed with Lewis, Bob McNamara, and Buddy Leake carrying the ball, and the team finished second to Edmonton with a 12-4 record.

After beating Calgary in the western semi-final, the Bombers snuffed out Edmonton's three-year reign, winning the final series 2-1. They won game three 17-2 in Edmonton with two overtime touchdowns, but came out of it with a rash of injuries that negated their prospects in the Grey Cup final against Hamilton.

It didn't help their cause when James broke a finger in the first quarter, and fumbled four times in the game. Ploen was bounced with a knee injury in the second half, and homebrew Barry Roseborough came in at quarterback and threw a touchdown pass to Dennis Mendyk for the only Bomber score in a 32-7 defeat

A GREY CUP DYNASTY IS BORN

The next five seasons were the high point in the club's history. The Big Blue machine steamrollered

KENNY PLOEN: THE WINNER

BY BOB PICKEN

The one dominant factor in the football career of Kenny Ploen was his ability to win—in high school, at the University of Iowa, and in guiding the Blue Bombers to four Grey Cup championships.

He grew up in the small midwestern city of Clinton, Iowa, and passed on a basketball scholarship at Kentucky to go to college in his home state, fulfilling a boyhood dream. He played both quarterback and defensive back for Iowa, an ability that made him invaluable later in the Bomber lineup.

Not much was expected of the Iowa Hawkeyes in Ploen's senior year. The school's football team never had won a Big Ten conference title prior to 1956. But they surprised everybody, beating Ohio State and Notre Dame, compiling an 8-1 record and earning a trip to the Rose Bowl.

Ploen led the Hawkeyes to a 35-19 victory over Oregon State, and was selected as the game's Most Valuable Player. He completed nine of ten passes, one for a touchdown, and scored another on a 49-yard run.

■ Grey Cup champion quarterback Ken Ploen: *The sweet taste of success.*

Winnipeg Free Press

Looking back, Kenny said the atmosphere in the Rose Bowl stadium in Pasadena was incomparable. "Over a hundred thousand people watching, a beautiful facility, the parade in the morning, the reaction of our Iowa fans afterward, it's something I will never forget."

Ploen knew his passing record would not attract interest from the NFL, but Bomber coach Bud Grant thought his talents were ideal for Canadian football, and offered him a contract in 1957. Part of the deal was an industrial engineer's position off the field.

He joined the Bombers to start an 11-year career, and likely was one of the few players ever to be a starter in both a Rose Bowl and a Grey Cup game in the same year. He was not a winner both times, however, as the Bombers were belted 32-7 by the Tiger-Cats in Toronto.

Ploen was one of many Iowa graduates recruited by Grant. He followed Calvin Jones (killed in a plane crash after the all-star game in Vancouver in December 1956), and was joined by Frank Rigney, Bill Whisler, Frank Gilliam, and Sherwyn Thorson.

He had many high points in the Bomber years, uppermost the four Grey Cup titles in five years from 1958 to 1962. Often overlooked was his all-star selection as a defensive back in 1959, the year he made 10 pass interceptions before returning to the quarterback position late in the season.

He also is renowned for two spectacular plays. "Yes, the overtime touchdown run to beat the Tiger-Cats in 1961 was special, and I guess that pass to Nielsen (109 yards, pass-and-run, 1965 western final) at McMahon Stadium is still in the CFL playoff record book."

Ploen passed for 16,470 yards in his Bomber career, with an excellent pass completion average of 56 per cent. He is one of the team's most celebrated heroes from its most successful era, and very deservingly, was inducted into the Canadian Football Hall of Fame in 1975.

Another decision has endeared him to Winnipeg. He and wife Jan moved here, sank their roots, and raised their family in the city. He rejected an offer to move to Vancouver when his playing days were over, and still lives in Winnipeg, a pillar of our community.

Bob Picken is a veteran CBC sports broadcaster.

across the west with first place records of 13-3, 12-4, 14-2, 13-3, and 11-5 from 1958 to '62. Only in 1960 did the Bombers fail to win the West and the Grey Cup, and ironically, that was the year when the team was rated at its peak.

The 1958 Cup final against the Tiger-Cats, played before 34,426 in Vancouver's Empire Stadium, was a classic. Michigan graduate Jim Van Pelt had replaced the injured Ploen at quarterback part way through the season, and he delivered a sparkling performance in the final.

It didn't look like Winnipeg's day early in the first quarter. The Bombers fell behind 14-0 on two Hamilton touchdowns, one of them on a 75-yard run by Ralph Goldston after a fumble recovery. The play that put the Bombers back in the game was a halfback option pass by Lewis. He started to the right at the Hamilton 20-yard-line with sweep action, then braked, and passed back in the left flat to a wide open Van Pelt for the touchdown.

Van Pelt went on to score another touchdown, and booted two field goals and four converts for 22 points. Shepard ran for 120 yards and outpunted Hamilton's Cam Fraser. Rauhaus blocked a Fraser kick and recovered it in the end zone for another major. The Tiger-Cats appeared to lose control of the game after Goldston, one of their key defensive stalwarts, was ejected for punching Lewis, a charge he denied vehemently.

The final score was 35-28 for Winnipeg, and the Bombers were back in the Grey Cup throne room for the first time since 1941. They came home to a tumultuous welcome from celebrating fans, who roared their delight in the Winnipeg Arena. Hamilton coach Jim Trimble had predicted his team would "waffle" the Bombers, and led by Bomber booster Cliff Gardner, the crowd sang the parody "hang down your head Jim Trimble" with great gusto.

The script was different but the result was similar in 1959. After disposing of the Eskimos two

Winnipeg Tribune, University of Manitoba Archives

■ (From left) Ken Ploen and Dave Raimey, 1966: *The heart of the Bomber offence.*

SHORT YARDAGE

Did you know: The 1962 Grey Cup in Toronto, know as 'the Fog Bowl', was the first and only time a CFL game was played over a period of two days—Saturday, December 1 and Sunday, December 2. The fog became so thick during the game that the final 9 minutes and 29 seconds had to be played the next day. Blue Bombers defeated Hamilton 28-27.

Archives of Manit

straight in the western final, the Bombers topped the Tiger-Cats 21-7 at CNE Stadium in Toronto. The leadership roles were reversed, as Ploen was back at quarterback after an injury to Van Pelt moved him to the Bomber defensive team.

The Bombers trailed 7-3 after three quarters, but erupted in the fourth after Tinsley recovered a Gerry McDougall fumble. Ploen hit Funston on a 40-yard pass that set up a Shepard touchdown, and fired a 33-yard TD strike to Pitts that clinched it. Another offensive weapon Grant used was the quick kick by fullback Shepard on second down, and he booted four singles over the heads of Hamilton defensive backs.

So, what happened in 1960? "That was a travesty," said Herbie Gray, who won a Schenley award that season as the league's outstanding defensive player. "We dominated the regular season, and did everything right until the western final against Edmonton."

The Eskimos finished eight points behind the Bombers, and lost three out of four meetings, but they gathered momentum by whipping Calgary in the semi-final. The teams split the first two games of the best-of-three series, but Ploen broke a bone in his hand in the process and that became a key factor when they met in the showdown at Winnipeg Stadium.

It wasn't much of football game, unless you get your kicks from defence. The offensive teams were stifled, and late in the fourth quarter the Bombers were nursing a 2-1 lead and trying to run out the clock. Ploen called a quarterback keeper on a third down short yardage play, but fumbled at his own 30-yard-line and the Eskimos recovered. Edmonton capitalized when Tommy-Joe Coffey booted a winning field goal for a shocking 4-2 upset. There were buckets of tears and the scene in the post-game Winnipeg dressing room was akin to a morgue.

The Bombers vowed to avenge that setback in 1961, the year the CFL started an east-west interlocking schedule, and that season another colourful personality arrived in Winnipeg. "Tricky Dicky" Thornton became a three-time all-star defensive back, but also took his turn at quarterback during a six-year period as a Blue Bomber.

Thornton was loquacious and flamboyant, popular with fans and the media, and a persistent self-booster. Former public address announcer Moe Renaud tells the tale of how after he punctuated a key Thornton interception with the comment "and Tricky Dicky does it again," Renaud was chastised by coach Grant.

"That's the last time I want to hear something like that, Moe," ordered Grant. "Thornton is enough of a hot dog anyway, without you adding some mustard to it."

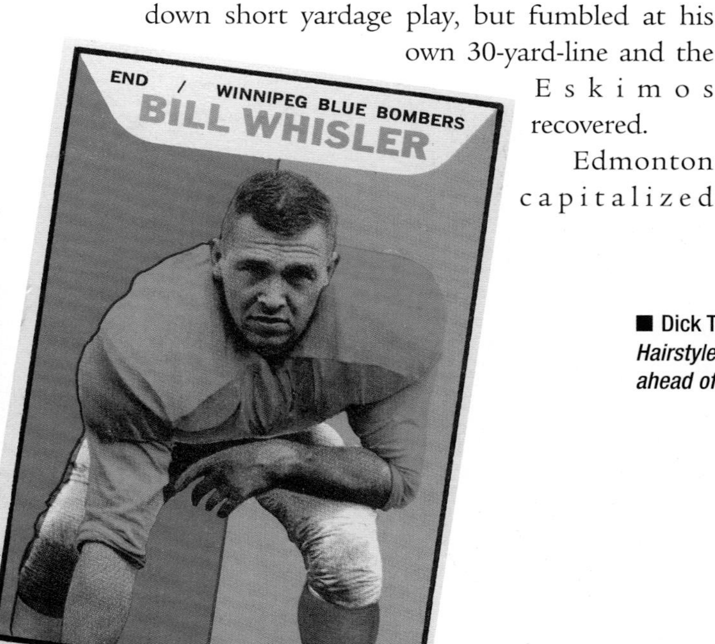

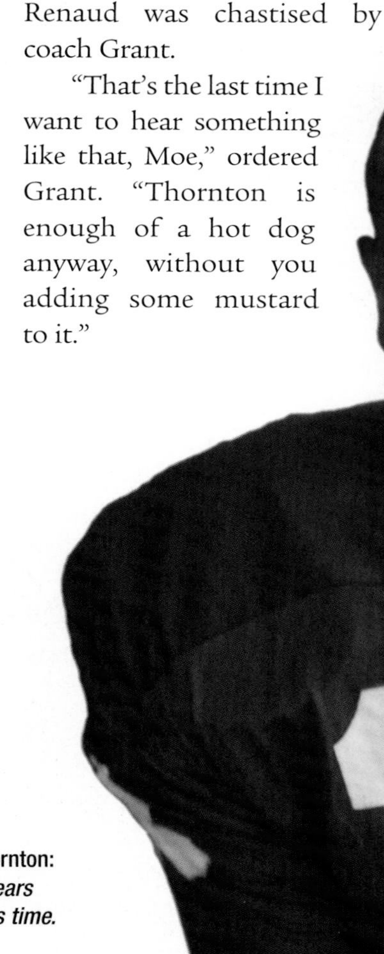

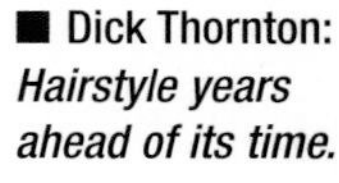

■ Dick Thornton: *Hairstyle years ahead of its time.*

Archives of Manitoba

Archives of Manitoba

■ (Above) Young Blue Bomber fans circa 1958.

■ (Right) Gerry James: *Along with father Eddie 'Dynamite' James, the only father-son duo in the Canadian Football Hall of Fame.*

The Bombers faced a new opponent in the western final of '61. Calgary upset Edmonton by the slender margin of one point in the two-game total-point semi-final. The Stampeders were no match for the Bombers, however, and were battered two straight, 14-1 and 43-14 in the final.

The Big Blue renewed their Grey Cup rivalry with the Tiger-Cats, but needed to go into overtime to win 21-14. It was a bitterly-fought game in the trenches as Lewis, James, and Roger Hagberg combined for 268 yards rushing to offset 25 pass completions by Hamilton's Bernie Faloney.

Deadlocked 14-14 after regulation time, the teams went into two 10-minute overtime periods. Ploen etched his name indelibly into the CFL record book with the winning play in the second session. He drove the Bombers to the Hamilton 19-yard-line, and called for a pass to Funston.

"I looked for Fungy but he was well covered," recalled Ploen. "I remember rolling out to the right, and suddenly I had some room to run. I was able to beat one of their tacklers around the 10-yard-line, and that was it, there I was in the end zone."

The Bombers and Tiger-Cats authored more historic CFL notes in 1962, but Calgary observers suggest the Big Blue got the largest break since creation on Harvey Wylie's faux pas in the third game of the western final.

All three games in the series were close, and the Stampeders were clinging to a 7-6 lead when the Bombers marched to the Calgary 17-yard-line in the dying moments of the finale. With time for just one play, Grant called for a field goal by James.

The kick was partially blocked by Calgary's Jim Furlong, and deflected wide of the posts and into the end zone where it spun to a halt in front of Wylie, the Stampeder safety. He could have simply dropped on the ball to concede a tying point forcing overtime, but instead elected to try to kick the ball from where it lay back into the field of play and out of bounds.

The result was disastrous for Calgary. Wylie flubbed the kick, it bounced a few yards forward, directly to the Bombers' Funston, who pounced on it for the winning touchdown in a 12-7 decision. The ecstatic crowd surged onto the field at

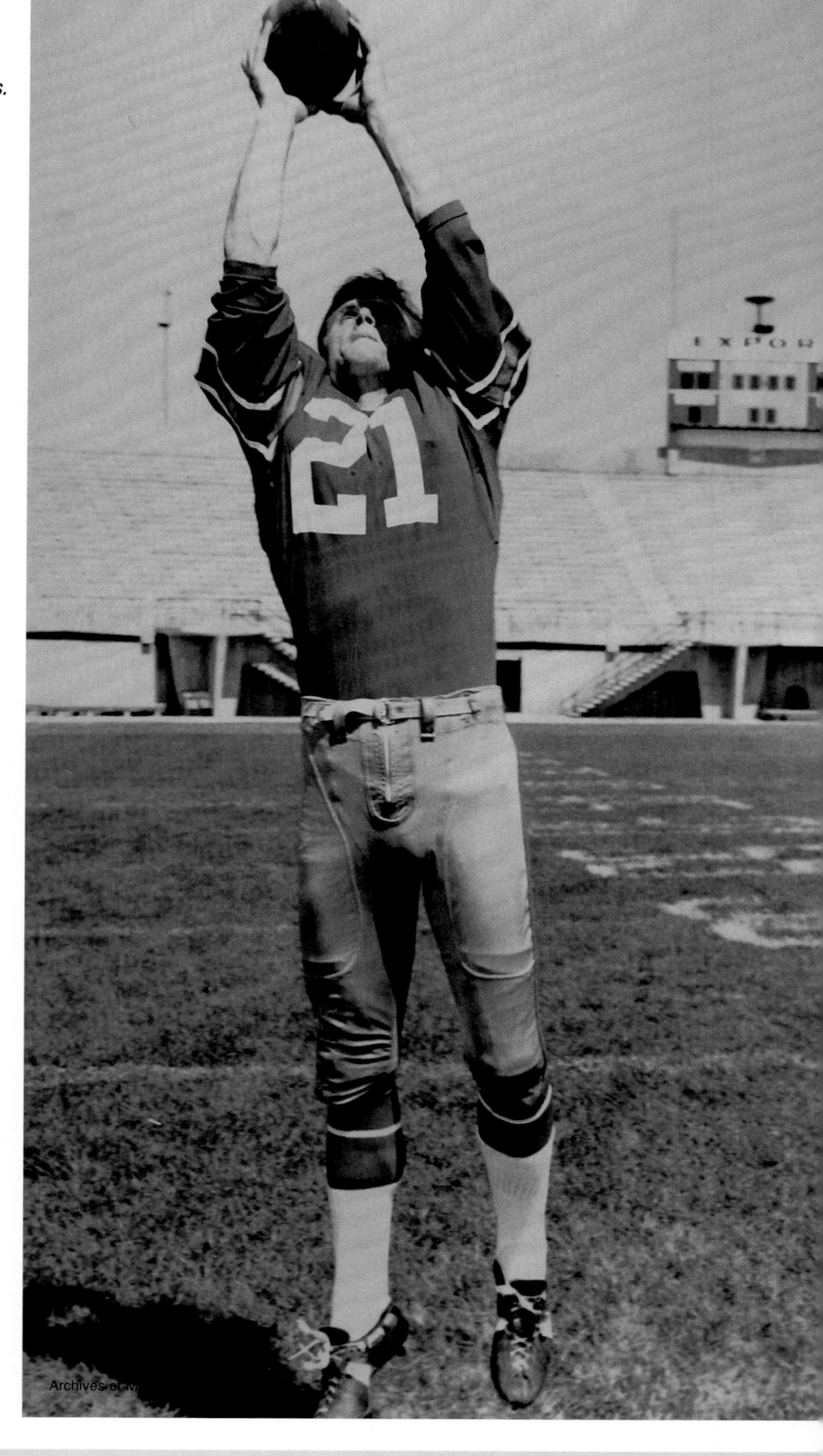

■ **Ken Nielsen, 1967:** ***Displayed speed, quickness and great hands.***

Winnipeg Stadium, and nobody thought about a convert as he Bombers won the West again.

The '62 Grey Cup final has been referred to ever since as the 'Fog Bowl.' A mixture of cool water in Lake Ontario and unusually high temperatures (48 degrees Fahrenheit) in Toronto that day, December 1st, produced waves of heavy fog over CNE Stadium on the lakeshore.

For most of the game the players had acceptable visibility, but not the fans, and the upper level television cameras were useless. Officials allowed it to continue until CFL commissioner Syd Halter called a halt with nine minutes and 29 seconds left in the fourth quarter, and ordered a continuation from that point the next day.

The Bombers were leading 28-27 on two touchdowns apiece by Lewis and Shepard at the point of suspension, and that was to be the final score. Over fifteen thousand fans came back for the Sunday portion, and watched the Winnipeg defensive unit hold the Tiger-Cats at bay for the fourth straight time in the national final.

The next two seasons, and the rest of the decade, were essentially a slide from the penthouse to the outhouse for the Bombers. The B.C. Lions ruled the western roost in 1963 and 1964, while Winnipeg teams missed the playoffs both years, and plunged into the ignominy of their worst season ever in '64, one win, 14 losses, and a tie.

Grant did an overhaul for the '65 season, cutting veterans like Hagberg and Warren, and augmenting his running game with Dave Raimey from Cleveland Browns and Art "Pearly" Perkins from Los Angeles Rams. He added an excellent Canadian flanker in Ken Nielsen, and assistant coach Michels created the highly effective 3-M

SHORT YARDAGE

Did you know: November 20, 1965, Ken Ploen and Ken Nielsen connected on a 109 yard pass and run play for a touchdown establishing the record for the longest pass and run play in CFL playoff history—a record that can only be tied.

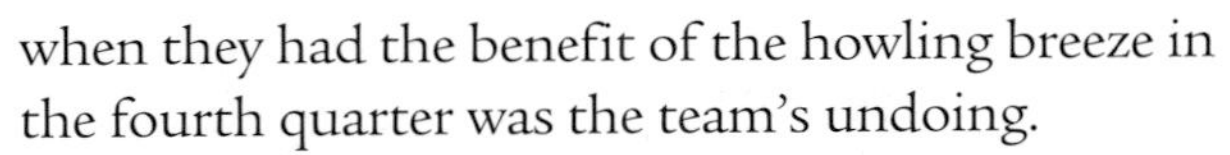

linebacking corps, with Phil Minnick, Ken Maglicic, and Al Miller.

It paid off as the Bombers rebounded for a second place 11-5 season, beat Saskatchewan in the western semi-final, and advanced to meet Calgary in the final. Former Bomber Eagle Day had surfaced with the Stampeders, and his passing gave them a 27-9 victory to open the best-of-three series.

HENRY JANZEN WINNIPEG BLUE BOMBERS

But Ploen and Lewis were into the twilight zone of their careers, and they had one more salvo to fire. They combined for a winning touchdown pass in a game two 14-11 win. Then in the third game, a stunned McMahon Stadium crowd in Calgary watched Ploen hit Nielsen for a 109-yard pass-and-run touchdown that beat the Stampeders 19-12.

FRANK RIGNEY WINNIPEG BLUE BOMBERS

The Bombers packed their bags for another Grey Cup game in Toronto, but the 1965 edition was to be their last appearance for 19 years. Like the Mud Bowl and the Fog Bowl, it also had bizarre conditions, this time engendered by gusty 40-mile-an-hour winds that forced officials to eliminate the no-yards penalty on punts.

Bomber kicker Ed Ulmer, normally one of the best in the league, had a nightmare in the afternoon. On one punt, the ball blew right back into his face, and caromed into the arms of Hamilton's John Barrow. Grant conceded three safety touches going into the wind, and they proved to be the margin of victory in favour of the Tiger-Cats, 22-16.

Lewis and Perkins scored Bomber touchdowns in the "Wind Bowl," but the failure of the offense to produce more than a Norm Winton field goal when they had the benefit of the howling breeze in the fourth quarter was the team's undoing.

The Grant-Michels era ended in Winnipeg after the 1966 season. The Bombers finished second with an 8-7-1 record, and defeated Edmonton in the semi-final. But '66 belonged to Saskatchewan, and after bouncing the Bombers two straight, the Roughriders went on to win their first Grey Cup title.

In the winter that followed, Grant received an offer he couldn't refuse from Minnesota, and he shifted to the Vikings taking Michels with him to develop an NFL powerhouse and more glory years in the Twin Cities. He could have gutted the coaching staff by removing Zaleski as well, but Black Magic relunctantly agreed to remain with the remnants of the team.

The competitive heart of the squad was fast fading. Lewis and Funston retired and Perkins departed. Ploen, Rigney and Piper played one more season. Zaleski still had Raimey, Nielsen, Pitts, and an all-star lineman in Bill Whisler, but the Bombers now were on a downhill toboggan.

The sixties ended with three years of lacklustre football, out of the playoffs, a record of 10-37-1, dead last in 1968 and '69, and dwindling attendance at Winnipeg Stadium.

The club needed a corporate fund-raising drive to get its finances back on an even keel, and it needed a stout hand on the management tiller. The man who filled the bill was Earl Lunsford, the former "Earthquake" of the Calgary Stampeders, who carried the ball for over a mile, 1,794 yards, in 1961.

Lunsford assumed the Bomber general manager's post in 1968, and while he couldn't produce a champion, he was a forthright businessman. He paid the bills, put fans back in the seats, and wrote the club's annual balance statements in black ink for the next 15 years. ■

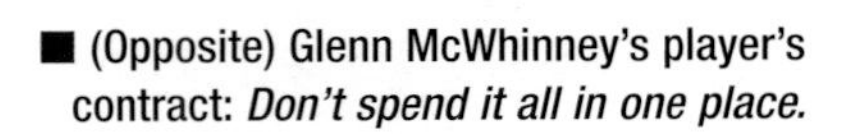

■ (Opposite) Glenn McWhinney's player's contract: *Don't spend it all in one place.*

WESTERN INTERPROVINCIAL FOOTBALL UNION

STANDARD PLAYER'S CONTRACT

BETWEEN

........XXXXXXXX WINNIPEG RUGBY FOOTBALL CLUB .... a member of the Western Interprovincial Football Union, which is an affiliate of the Canadian Rugby Union,

hereinafter called the "Club"

— and —

........GLENN S. McWHINNEY........................ of the ....City........ of ....Winnipeg........

in the ....Province........ of ....Manitoba........

hereinafter called the "Player"

In consideration of the mutual and respective covenants and agreements hereinafter contained, the parties hereto hereby agree as follows:

1. The term of this contract shall be from the date of execution hereof until the 1st day of June following the close of the football season commencing in 195..6...., subject however to rights of prior termination as specified herein.

2. The player agrees that during the term of this contract he will play football and will engage in activities related to football only for the Club and will play in all Western Interprovincial Football Union scheduled and play-off games, Canadian Rugby Union play-off games and any exhibition games for which the Club may arrange; and the Club, subject to the provisions hereof, agrees during such period to employ the player as a skilled football player. The player agrees during the term of this contract to report promptly for the Club's training seasons and at the Club's directions to participate in all practice sessions.

3. For the player's services as a skilled football player during the term of this contract, and for his agreement not to play football, or engage in activities relating to football, for any other person, firm, club or corporation during the term of this contract, and for the option hereinafter set forth giving the Club the right to renew this contract, and for the other undertakings of the Club herein, the Club promises to pay the player the sum of $ 5,000.00 ...., to be payable as follows:

75% of said salary in weekly instalments commencing with the first and ending with the last regularly scheduled league game played by the Club during such season and the balance of 25% of said sum at the end of the last scheduled league game, unless the Club shall, after the last scheduled league game, have any Western Interprovincial Football Union or Canadian Rugby Union play-off games to engage in, in which event the remaining 25% shall be paid at the end of the last of such play-off games.

See also paragraphs 24 and 25

4. The Club shall be entitled to deduct from each payment hereunder any amount required by the Government of Canada for Income Tax.

5. The Club agrees to pay the proper and necessary travelling and reasonable board and lodging expenses whenever the player is travelling in the services of the Club for games in other than the Club's home city, but when not so travelling, the player shall pay his own expenses.

6. Prior to the start of each football season, the player shall attend before the Club's medical committee for a complete physical and medical examination, and, if, in the opinion of the said medical committee, the player is not completely fit to participate in football activities, this agreement and everything herein contained, shall be, at the Club's option, void and of no force and effect.

7. The player agrees to comply with all the rules and regulations now, or which may hereafter be, adopted during the duration of this contract, by the Canadian Rugby Union and/or the Western Interprovincial Football Union and/or the Club.

■ Quarterback Don Jonas: *Loved to throw the deep ball and could run when he had to.*

CHAPTER 3

Archives of Manitoba

RETURN TO RESPECTABILITY

BY BOB IRVING

When club president Paul Quinton and general manager Earl Lunsford, better known as "Okie," hired Jim Spavital as head coach in 1970, it was supposed to signal the start of better days, a decade that would return the Bombers to the good times after what were often referred to as the "dark days" of Joe Zaleski. In fairness to Zaleski, he had the thankless, if not impossible, task of taking over an aging Bomber team that was in serious decline at the end of the Bud Grant era.

Spavital had played for the Bombers in 1951 and the Oklahoma State product, who everybody called "Spav," came to Winnipeg after two years as an assistant coach in Saskatchewan. Spavital was a task-master but his drill-sergeant's mentality didn't produce immediate results. His first year at the helm turned out to be a sorry reminder of what had preceded it. As a matter of

■ General Manager Earl Lunsford: *'Grab grass and growl'.*

Western Canada Pictorial Index

fact it was worse. The Bombers won only two games in 1970.

There was a ray of hope though. The Bombers lost seven of their 14 games by six points or fewer. Their problem was a dreadful offence. The Bombers scored a woeful 184 points in their 16 games in 1970 and in 10 of those games they scored 11 points or less. Lunsford and Spavital knew that the dilemma was rooted in the lack of a top-flight quarterback. Replacing the great Kenny Ploen after his retirement at the end of the 1967 season had proven to be a most difficult task. John Schneider tried in 1968 and 1969. Wally Gabler, Ron Johnson and Benji Dial in 1970 weren't the answer either. Finding a quarterback who could breathe some life into their stagnant attack became the mission for Okie and Spav and they found an answer thanks to one of the best short-term moves in Bomber history.

■ **Tuufuli Uperesa:** *Needless to say, he wore the biggest helmet on the club.*

THE BEST DEFENCE IS A GOOD OFFENCE

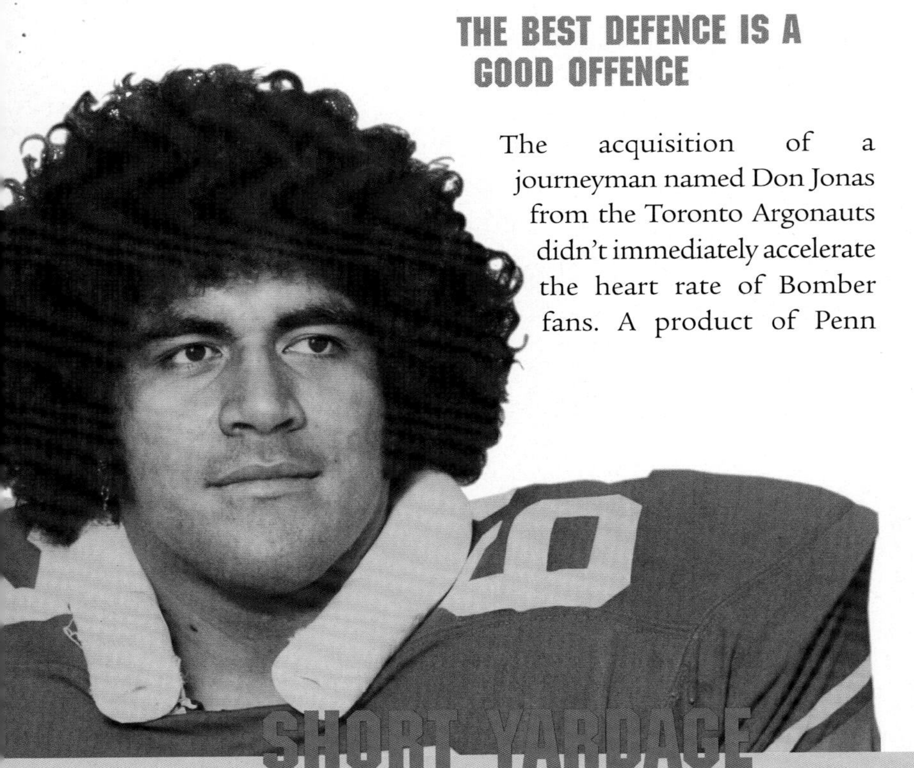

The acquisition of a journeyman named Don Jonas from the Toronto Argonauts didn't immediately accelerate the heart rate of Bomber fans. A product of Penn State, Jonas was 30, he had bounced from the Philadelphia Eagles to the Continental League and then the Argos. But, Jonas was a perfect fit for the sophisticated run-and-shoot style offence installed by innovative offensive coach Dave Smith. When the Bombers added Mack Herron and Jim Thorpe to an attack that already included Ed Williams, University of Manitoba rookie Bob Kraemer, Bob Larose, Paul Markle, Bill Frank and Bob Swift, among others, their moribund attack suddenly grew wings and began to soar.

Jonas was the fulcrum, however unconventional. Larose used to joke about a favourite play Jonas would often call when the Bombers got into what is known as the "red zone" (inside the opponents 20-yard line). The instruction in the huddle was a simple "70-A.G.O." Translated, it meant "anybody get open." It was about as sandlot as you could get, but it worked. With his ad-lib, confident, approach, Jonas ran Smith's offence just the way the coach wanted. Not only did Jonas produce on the field, his charismatic and swashbuckling style allowed him to take Winnipeg by storm off the field as well. There wasn't a cause Jonas wouldn't support, a baby he wouldn't kiss, a hand he wouldn't shake, a cigar he wouldn't smoke. He was everywhere.

The Bombers improved dramatically to 7-8-1 in 1971, they led the CFL in points scored and Jonas was number one in the league in completions, 253, passing yards, 4,036, touchdowns, 27, and in points scored with 121 (he also did the team's placekicking). To top it off, he became the first Blue Bomber to ever win the CFL's Most Outstanding Player award. The season didn't end well as the Bombers lost the west semi-final 34-23 to Saskatchewan but thanks to Jonas and his

SHORT YARDAGE

Did you know: 1970s Offensive lineman Tuufuli Uperesa amused and terrified fellow teammates on a duck hunting trip by shooting shotgun pellets just above their heads. No one ever went hunting with him again.

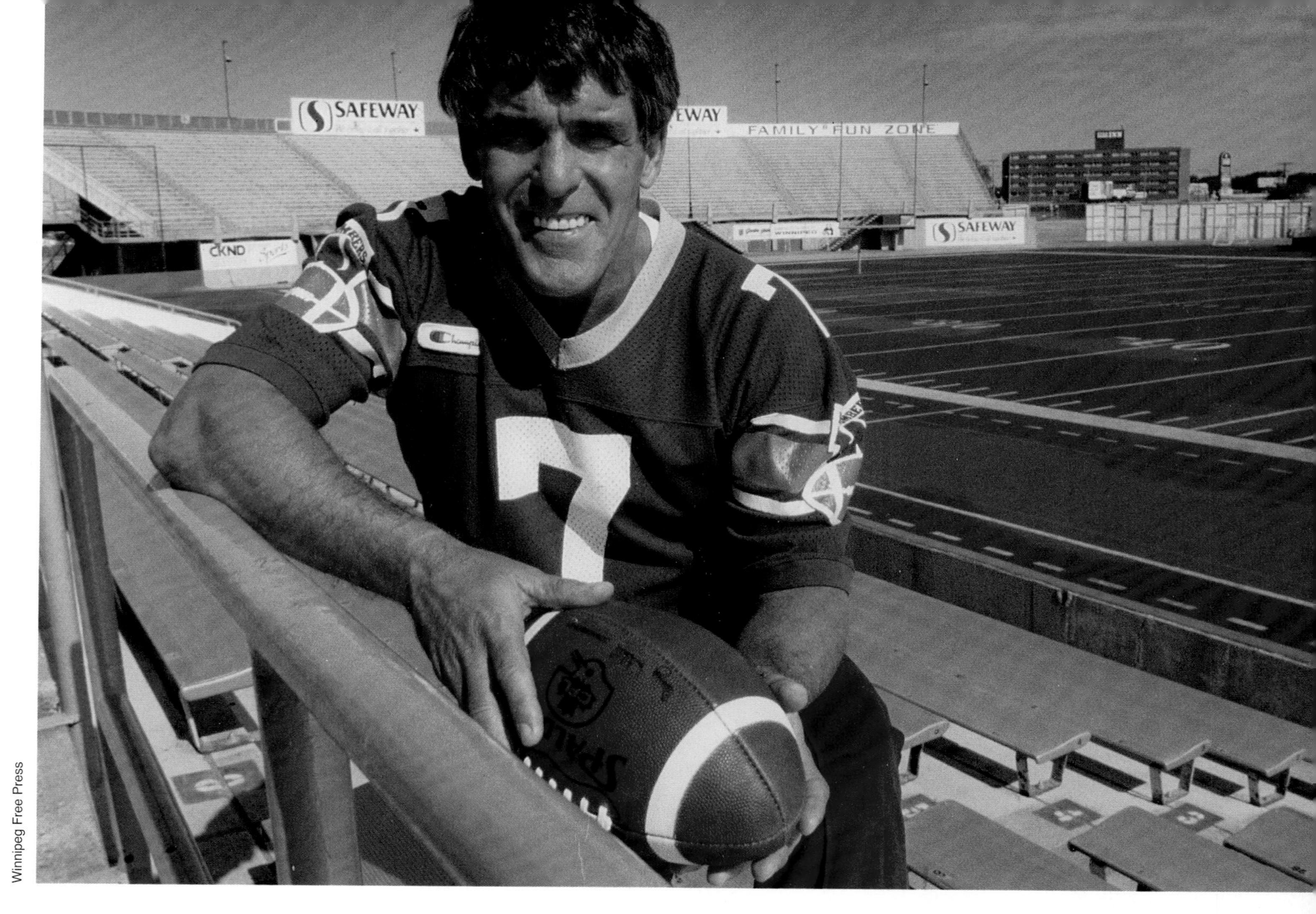

Winnipeg Free Press

supporting cast, Winnipeg was nuts about the Bombers again, the world was Mr. Jonas's oyster.

The 1972 season was even better. With Jonas and his flamboyant approach at the controls, and Herron and Thorpe blossoming into full-fledged stardom, the Bombers once again led the CFL in scoring, creating offensive excitement that hadn't been matched for a long time. Herron led the CFL in rushing with 1,559 yards, had a 120-yard kickoff return for a touchdown, and posted a stunning 32.5 yard kickoff return average. Thorpe caught 70 passes for 1,260 yards. He had a 97-yard touchdown bomb among his 11 receiving touchdowns. Jonas had another big year, throwing for 3,583 yards and 27 touchdowns in the 16-game season. Seven of the Bombers eight home games drew sellout crowds of 25,210 as the club broke all existing attendance records. A 10-6 record produced a first place finish and the right to host the western final against Saskatchewan. Not quite Utopia but the Bombers were definitely the talk of the town.

Unfortunately this exhilarating but brief period of Blue Bomber brilliance started to crumble in the west final. The Green and White Riders inflicted a crushing 27-24 loss on the Bombers in that game. It was a result that featured some questionable strategy by the Bombers and it's a loss that is still agonized over by Bomber fans. The collapse continued after the season ended. Both Herron and Thorpe were released as the dark side of their lifestyles became too troubling for the football club to put up with. Those moves, combined with the devastating setback by the Riders, signalled the beginning of the end for Jonas and

■ **Don Jonas:** *Never met a camera he didn't like.*

ED ULMER
BLUE BOMBERS
WINNIPEG
Blue Bombers
DEFENSIVE HALFBACK

■ **Captain Blue:** ***Flying the Blue Bomber.***

Spavital. In 1973, Jonas hadn't lost any of his swagger, but he had lost Herron and Thorpe. Without his two primary weapons, Jonas threw only 13 touchdown passes against 29 interceptions, and the Bombers scored 134 fewer points than the year before. Veteran stalwarts Joe Critchlow, Mickey Doyle, Rob McLaren, Gene Lakusiak, Phil Minnick and Chuck Harrison were at the end of the trail. The Bombers stumbled home with a 4-11-1 record that had the fans shaking their heads over how it could all fall apart so quickly. Jonas, off the strength of his two previous seasons, was given the benefit of the doubt, but at the end of the '73 season, Jim Spavital was asked to leave.

In 1974, Bud Riley became the third coach hired by Lunsford. Riley had spent 20 years coaching high school and college ball in the U.S. before putting in one year as an assistant coach in Saskatchewan. Riley favoured a style of offence that incorporated slotbacks, like rookie Tom Scott and local product Gord Paterson, heavily into the passing attack. To make it work, the coach needed a certain kind of quarterback. Riley stayed with Jonas at the start of the '74 season.

The team got off to an 0-3 start, but Jonas rallied them to three straight wins and all seemed to be right with the world. Or so everyone thought, except Riley and his coaches. They had grown weary of Jonas's propensity to freelance and make things up on the fly. When the Bombers returned home from Regina, where they had posted a 20-18 Labour Day win that evened their record at 3-3, Jonas was pulled aside in the airport and informed that he had been traded. It was one of the oddest bits of timing in club history. To quote Walt Mckee "the guys were really surprised at that one." Thus ended one of the most mercurial careers in Bomber history. Jonas almost single-handedly revitalized the Blue Bomber franchise during the 1971 and '72 seasons with his daring play and his electric personality. Such was his impact that Jonas was given much of the credit for a stadium expansion in 1972 that pushed capacity to 25,210. His fall from favour was as stunning as his rise to stardom. Jonas was sent to Hamilton for the much younger Chuck Ealey, who at 24 was two years removed from leading the Ticats to a Grey Cup win as a rookie. A memorable, yet surprisingly brief era, ended suddenly, stunningly.

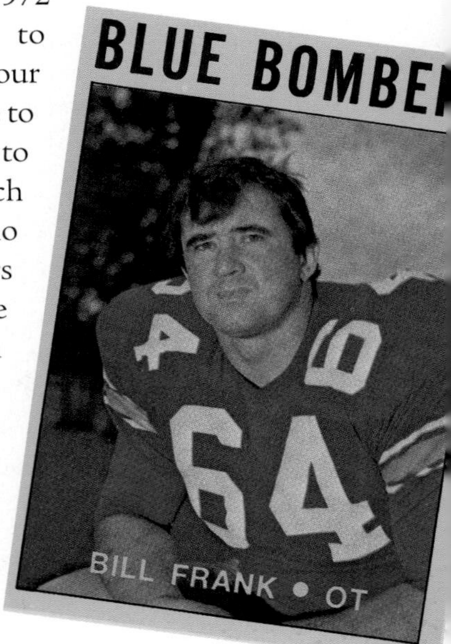

BAD BOYS: MACK HERRON AND JIM THORPE

BY BOB IRVING

When the 1971 CFL season began, Blue Bomber fans were not only starved for victories, they had also developed a voracious appetite for some much-needed excitement. A pair of new recruits named Mack Herron and Jim Thorpe would bring plenty of that, both on and off the field.

Thorpe spent the 1969 and 1970 seasons with the Toronto Argonauts before the Bombers acquired his rights. He was coming off an All-Canadian season in which he had posted a phenomenal 27.8 average on 26 catches. At 6-foot-1, 195 pounds, Thorpe was a stud, a big target with tremendous speed. His roomate, kicker Walt Mckee, remembers Thorpe as cocky and abrasive, not to mention a "tremendous talent." Mckee says Thorpe was also one of the first real "trash-talkers" in the CFL, always telling his opponents how much trouble they were in for.

Herron was an undersized running back, 5-foot-5, 180 pounds, who had set 10 Kansas State football records. He had tremendous quickness and claimed to run the "100" in a blistering 9.4 seconds. Mckee says Herron was "amazing, his quickness was unbelievable." Paul Robson, a former linebacker and long-snapper with the Bombers, said Herron was "surprisingly tough, hard-nosed, for someone so small. When he hit the line, it was a sight to behold."

Blue Bomber GM Earl Lunsford and Coach Jim Spavital knew that Thorpe and Herron brought some baggage, and had troubled pasts. But the Bombers were desperate to upgrade their offensive talent and decided to take a chance.

On the field Thorpe and Herron didn't disappoint. If anything they were better than expected. Thorpe caught 70 passes for 1,436 yards in 1971 and followed it up with another 70 catches for 1,260 yards in 1972. Herron rushed for 900 yards in his rookie season, then broke loose for a league-leading 1,559 yards rushing in 1972. Mini-Mack, as he was called, also caught 39 passes for 451 yards that second year and posted a staggering 32.5 yard average on kickoff returns. Along with Don Jonas, Thorpe and Herron turned the Bomber offence into one of the most feared and dangerous in the CFL. The excitement Bomber fans were craving was delivered game after game.

■ Mack Herron: *Before Charles Roberts, there was "Mini" Mack.*

Off the field, things weren't quite so good. Mckee remembers Thorpe and Herron shared a house together and the players on the team "kept hearing rumours that the two were up to no good." Robson, who was teaching school along with playing for the Bombers, says "I heard persistent rumours from kids I was teaching. Some of them claimed they were partying with Herron and Thorpe." It was, of course, much more than just "partying." Suffice it to say it was a bad scene all around, and at the end of the 1972 season Lunsford and the club's executive, on the urging of local police, decided Herron and Thorpe were more trouble than they were worth. Despite their unparalleled ability, their sensational contributions over the previous two years and their enormous value to the team, both players were released.

Thorpe's football career sputtered and quickly ended while Herron went on to success in the NFL before running afoul of the law and spending much of his post-football life in prison.

Bob Irving is sports director of CJOB 68 radio.

DIETER BROCK: THE BIRMINGHAM RIFLE

BY PAUL FRIESEN

The 13-year-old boy leaned in closer to the radio, intent on hearing every word from the announcer, every cheer from the crowd and every sound from the field.

This is how heroes are born, in a kid's room in a house at the end of a dead-end street alongside the railway tracks in a small, Manitoba town.

The hero coming to life that day was a soft-spoken, strong-armed quarterback from Birmingham, Alabama named Ralph Brock.

It was 1975, and Brock had come off the bench to spark the Winnipeg Blue Bombers, a team the boy knew only through the tiny speaker on his radio and those glorious stories in the newspaper.

The boy, of course, had no idea what role the quarterback, the radio or the newspaper would play in his life, years later. He knew only that the player wearing No. 5 that day was something special.

By the end of the 1975 season, most of Winnipeg knew it, too. And on October 5, Bomber head coach Bud Riley made Brock his starting quarterback, replacing Chuck Ealey, for a game at the Autostad in Montreal.

That decision launched one of the most exciting eras in Blue Bomber history, as the man with the golden arm and the southern drawl passed his way into the record books.

By the time the footballs had stopped flying, Brock would be a two-time winner of the CFL's most outstanding player award and the franchise's all-time leading passer.

As the Brock legend grew, so did the boy, eating it all up the way a teenager devours dinner. He knew, for instance, that Brock spent off-seasons throwing weighted footballs into a mattress propped against his rec room wall in Birmingham. How Brock was so strong he could throw a ball through the uprights from 50 yards away, while on his knees. And how he could win arm-wrestling contests with offensive and defensive linemen. The boy saw that one with his own eyes during a skills and strength competition shown at halftime on TV.

By the late 1970s, though, public opinion had begun to turn against his hero. The Brock's a Crock faction argued that the quarterback hadn't taken the Bombers to a Grey Cup. And when Ralph said he'd prefer to be called Dieter, his middle name, well, that sent some people over the deep end.

■ Dieter Brock: *Nobody ever did it better…throw the football that is.*

Winnipeg Free Press

Winnipeg Free Press

So the boy wrote Brock a letter one winter, telling him to ignore the critics. 484 Turtle Creek Drive, Birmingham, Alabama was an address the kid will probably never forget. Just like he won't forget the Christmas card that arrived in response, thanking him for his support.

In 1980, Brock fans were vindicated, to some extent, as he won the first of back-to-back outstanding player awards. But still, no Grey Cup.

So when Brock staged a training camp holdout to back his demands for a new contract in 1983, many fans were ready to run him out of town. New head coach Cal Murphy was happy to oblige, and on September 20, Brock was traded to Hamilton for quarterback Tom Clements.

The boy was a man by now, but heroes die hard. So when the Tiger-Cats visited the Bombers, he wasn't one of those who yelled 'Brockbusters!' from the stands.

And when the two teams met in the '84 Grey Cup, he couldn't help but smile when Brock's touchdown run gave the Ticats an early, 14-point lead.

The Bombers would end a 22-year Grey Cup drought that day, and Brock would go on to play a season in the NFL, before retiring. Six years later, he was named to the Bomber Hall of Fame.

That's when the boy finally met his hero, at the same radio station he used to listen to as a 13-year-old, where he now trained as a student journalist.

He didn't know it at the time, but the woman who introduced him to his hero would turn out to be his wife, another lifelong member of the Diet's a Treat club.

Five years later, at their wedding, the voice of Dieter Brock blared congratulations to Susan and Paul over the loudspeakers just before dinner.

The man who made that happen: the announcer who, through a radio speaker in 1975, told the boy all about No. 5.

Brock has long since moved on from 484 Turtle Creek Drive, the Bombers and the CFL. But when the boy, now a sportswriter, saw a chance to keep the legend alive in this book, he jumped at it.

Some heroes never die at all.

Paul Friesen is a football writer with the Winnipeg Sun.

THERE'S ALWAYS THE ZOO

Chuck Ealey played well enough for the rest of the '74 season, helping the Bombers recover to finish 8-8 and narrowly miss the playoffs. Ealey was number-one when the 1975 season began but he never really gained the trust of Riley. The coach was enamoured with a young signal-caller from Alabama, who had attended Auburn University and Jacksonville State. When Ealey turned in a particularly tepid performance during an October tie in Toronto, Riley couldn't wait any longer. The quarterbacking reins were handed over to a strong-armed gunslinger named Ralph Dieter Brock. Brock's debut was effective, if not sensational, as he led the Bombers to a 26-21 win in Montreal. The Bombers finished 6-8-2 in 1975 but Brock performed bravely during a 42-24 semi-final loss to Saskatchewan, and Riley was convinced he had found the quarterback that could lead the Bombers to a championship.

The 1976 and '77 seasons produced exciting, winning football. Operating behind an offensive line that was anchored by a pair of Brock's Alabama henchmen, Butch Norman and Buddy Brown, and sturdy Canadian veteran Chuck Liebrock, and with running backs Jim Washington and Richard Crump, along with receivers like Scott, Paterson, and Mike Holmes to throw it to, Brock started to become a force. The Bombers were pretty good on defence as well with defensive linemen Jim Heighton, Elton Brown, Dave Knechtel and local product Lyall Woznesensky, safety Brian Herosian, linebackers Bob Toogood and Harry Walters and defensive back Vince Phason leading the way.

The team finished 10-6 both years but when the playoffs rolled around, all they could produce was heartbreak. They finished second in 1976 and suffered a gut-wrenching 14-12 semi-final loss at home to Edmonton. In 1977, they wound up third, which resulted in a trip to B.C. for the semi-final and one of the toughest playoff losses in club history. In the waning moments of the game, Lions' defensive back Joe Fourqurean came out of nowhere to deflect a Brock bomb that was surely destined to land in the arms of a streaking Mike Holmes and give the Bombers the win at Empire Stadium. It was a dramatic play that is still talked about by CFL fans and it allowed the Lions to escape with a 33-32 victory. That loss, coupled with the fact Bud Riley had become embroiled in a feud with the two Winnipeg football writers, Jack Matheson of the *Tribune* and Don Blanchard of the *Free Press*, prompted GM Lunsford to decide it was time for yet another coaching change. This time Lunsford picked a former Bomber player to take charge.

Ray Jauch had been a running back with the Bombers in 1960 and '61, famous for his dogged determination and a blood-curdling yell that he emitted each time he carried the ball. He had subsequently become an accomplished coach, starting with the St. James Rods juniors in 1962 and progressing to a seven-year run as head coach of the Edmonton Eskimos which was capped by the 1975 Grey Cup championship. Unhappy with a management role he had been pushed into in Edmonton, Jauch jumped at Lunsford's invitation to return to Winnipeg and take over the Bombers. Jauch's arrival was hailed as the most legitimate coaching hire Lunsford had made during his long tenure as GM. Here was a man who had impeccable coaching credentials that included a championship, plus he was a former Bomber player. Surely glory was just around the next bend.

■ Bomber punt returner Michael Allen: *Taking one back against Saskatchewan.*

Jauch's debut met with generally good reviews. He presided over a 1978 Bomber team that had more than a few talented players. Perennial all-Canadian defensive tackle John Helton was acquired in a blockbuster trade with Calgary, Mike Holmes had become a game-breaker, Bernie Ruoff set a club record with 149 points, and a young sensation from the University of Alberta named Joe Poplawski won CFL rookie-of-the-year honours. The Bombers finished a respectable 9-7 before injuries led to disaster in the playoffs. A knee problem kept Brock out of the west semi-final in Calgary, number-two quarterback Terry Luck was also hurt, and with sore-armed Harry Knight calling the signals the Bombers had as much chance as a mosquito at a hummingbird convention—they were trampled 38-4 by the Stampeders.

Jauch's arrival was hailed as the most legitimate coaching hire Lunsford had made during his long tenure as GM.

Even though he had a competitive team, Jauch, who definitely operated under the 'my way or the highway' mantra, decided it was time to make wholesale changes, time to establish his team with his players. Jauch said a "fungus" had developed within the Bomber ranks, and in order to disinfect what he considered to be an unhealthy playing environment, some of the club's longest serving veteran players were soon on the way out. All-star centre Bob Swift, considered a solid team player and all-around good guy, had been let go in '78 and one of Jauch's most public feuds was with a player who was equally as stubborn as the head coach, Gord Paterson. The two were on different wavelengths, and when Paterson failed to emerge from the locker room after a half-time blowup with Jauch during a game in Edmonton, his Bomber days were over. Jauch had a mandate to do whatever he deemed necessary to build a championship contender and there was no room for sentimentality.

The ouster of many key players and a brutal string of injuries, including a broken ankle suffered by Poplawski, led to a disastrous 4-12 season in 1979, prompting many to wonder if Jauch was on the right track. The next three years would prove that clearly, he was. When the 1980 season began, Jauch had assembled an impressive array of talent. Brock had an offensive arsenal that was led up front by perennial all-stars Norman and Brown, along with emerging star centre John Bonk, Big Bobby Thompson and newly acquired Nick Bastaja. Receivers included Holmes, Poplawski, Eugene Goodlow and Rick House. A terrific rookie running back named William Miller arrived on the scene, as did a good Canadian fullback named Dan Huclack. The defence was led by stars like Helton, Toogood, James Reed, Tony Norman, Vince Phason, newly acquired Paul Bennett, Leo Ezerins, Charlie Williams and Reggie Pierson. Trevor Kennerd took over as the place-kicker, Bob Cameron as the punter, after Bernie Ruoff, famous for being flakey and wearing a wrist-watch during games, ran afoul of the marijuana police and was traded.

Over the next three years, this nucleus would deliver entertaining, high-scoring football to big crowds at Winnipeg Stadium. They went 10-6 in 1980, 11-5 in both '81 and '82. Unfortunately, their timing was lousy. Their hated rivals, the Edmonton Eskimos, were in the middle of a dynasty. Since 1978 they had produced a string of five consecutive Grey Cup victories. This Eskimos juggernaut featured some of the greatest players in CFL history, and as good as Jauch's Bombers were, they couldn't beat Hugh Campbell's Eskimos.

Winnipeg Free Press

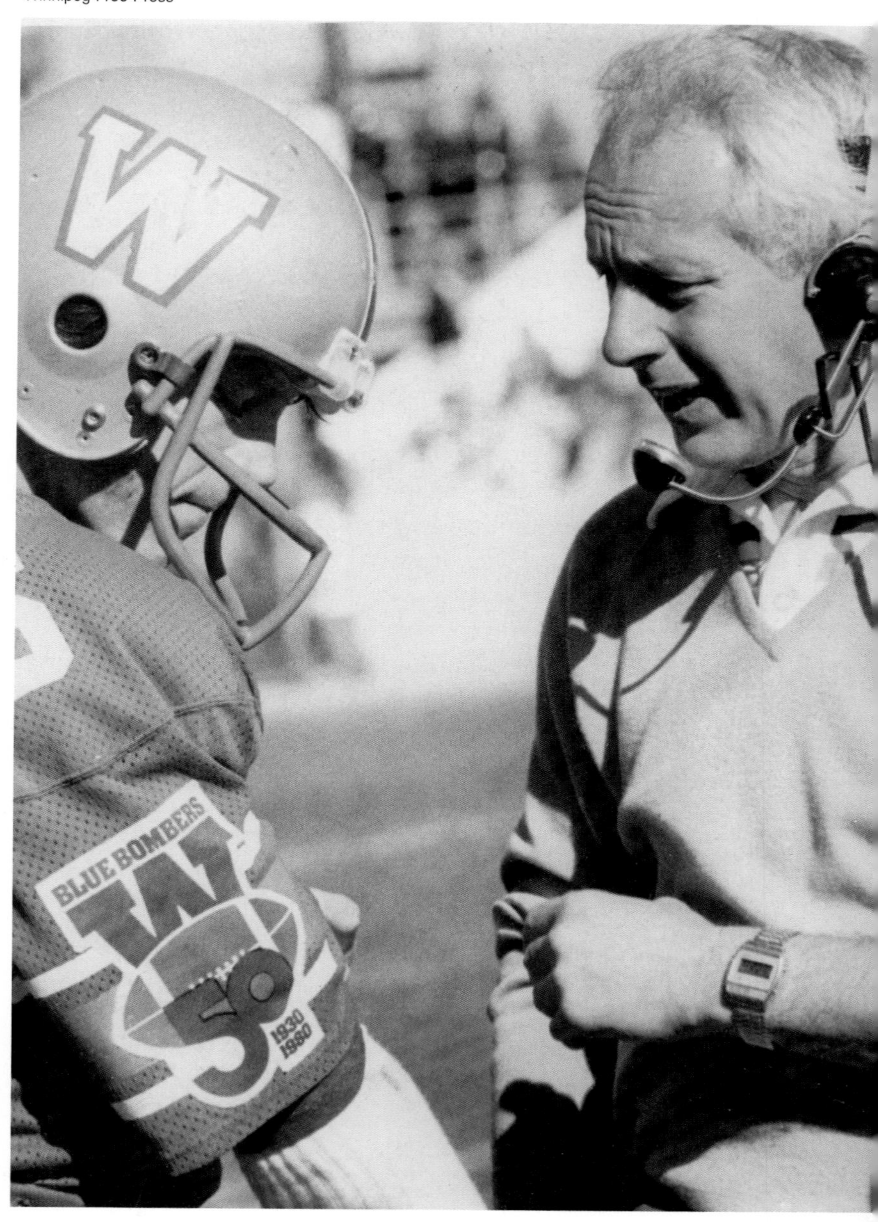

■ Head coach Ray Jauch: *Brought the Bombers back to winning ways in the early 1980s.*

SHORT YARDAGE

Did you know: 'Mini' Mack Herron voiced a series of radio spots for a Winnipeg car dealership, Motor Sales, and was given an Austin Mini to drive during his time as a Blue Bomber.

In 1980, the Bombers lost the West final 34-24 in Edmonton's brand new Commonwealth Stadium. The 1981 season featured a 58-2 win over ex-NFL star Vince Ferragamo and the Montreal Alouettes in front of 32,896 at Winnipeg Stadium and a six-game win streak to close the year. The team took tremendous momentum into the playoffs, only to see Brock and company have a bad day in the semi-final, losing 15-11 to B.C..

And in 1982, a Bomber team that had been strengthened by the addition of territorial protections Milson Jones and Stan Mikawos was once again playing the West final in Edmonton. The Bombers gave the mighty Eskimos the fight of their lives. It was a phenomenal football game, bitterly contested, brutally physical, and the Eskimos were able to hang on and win it 24-21. Another play Bomber fans still talk about and lament over was a controversial late game roughing the quarterback call against John Helton on Warren Moon that paved the way for the Eskimos to gain the victory.

That wasn't the only controversial aspect to the 1982 season. The other centred around Jauch. In one of the most unusual developments in Winnipeg Football Club history, Lunsford called a news conference early in the season to announce that Jauch had accepted a lucrative offer to become the coach of the Washington Federals of the fledgling United States Football League effective in 1983. Even though Lunsford, his assistant Paul Robson and club president George Graham were not happy about Jauch's situation, they decided that firing him would cause a major disruption within the ranks of their contending team. He was allowed to stay and coach the 1982 team.

It was at the end of Jauch's coaching tenure that the Bomber executive decided it was time to bring the curtain down on Earl Lunsford's 15-year reign as general manager. "Okie" had enjoyed a remarkably long run that featured equal amounts of regular season success and playoff disappointment. Lunsford was fired and replaced by his assistant, former Bomber player Paul Robson, the start of yet another new Bomber "era."

JOE POPLAWSKI: THE GOLDEN BOY

BY BOB IRVING

In 1978, Joe Poplawski was a 20-year-old student at the University of Alberta. He was pursuing a Bachelor of Sciences degree with the goal of getting into dentistry. But he was also a rapidly improving college placekicker and receiver who, at the time, had no idea how big a role football would play in his life.

Poplawski had attracted the attention of CFL teams with his natural athletic abilities. It was when he played in the 1978 Can-Am bowl that NFL scouts also took notice. They encouraged him to play a fourth year of University football which would make him eligible for the NFL draft. But, the hometown Edmonton Eskimos knew all about Poplawski's talent and potential and made him one of their territorial protections.

Having already been burned by losing another Edmonton native, receiver Bryan Fryer, to the NFL, the Eskimos invited Poplawski to a meeting at which Edmonton head coach Hugh Campbell advised Joe he was too slow and too small to make it in the NFL. Campbell "encouraged" Poplawski to sign with the Eskimos. Poplawski, on the suggestion of his university coach Jim Donlevy, hired an Edmonton lawyer named Ed Molstad to represent him. On Molstad's advice, Poplawski told Campbell that he was going to return to university and keep his NFL options open. Thirty minutes

■ **Joe Poplawski beating a Calgary defender:** ***Great routes, sure hands.***

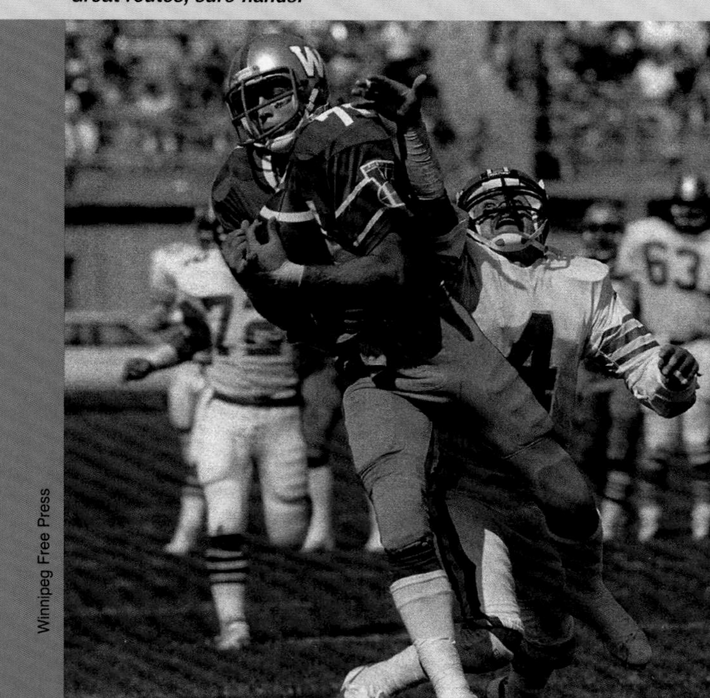
Winnipeg Free Press

after Poplawski left his meeting with Campbell, he received a call from Donlevy, who told him Eskimos General Manager Norm Kimball had phoned. Kimball, an arrogant man who didn't take rejection well, told Donlevy "We'll get even with that Poplawski." Two days later, football writer Ray Turchansky of the *Edmonton Journal* phoned Poplawski to tell him that he had been traded to the Winnipeg Blue Bombers for slotback Tom Scott. Poplawski never heard from the Eskimos again.

He did hear from Blue Bomber General Manager Paul Robson. Robson was anxious to have Poplawski come to training camp but Joe stuck to his plan, saying he was going to stay at the University of Alberta and pursue dentistry. The Bombers didn't give up, and after a few phone calls from head coach Ray Jauch, Poplawski asked Molstad to see what kind of contract he could negotiate. The Bombers offered a $15,000 salary with a $1,000 signing bonus. Molstad worked them up to $25,000 with a $5,000 bonus. Poplawski was starting to enjoy the negotiating game, and he recalls asking Molstad "Ed, do you think we can get more?" Molstad's reply was an emphatic "No." Poplawski accepted the offer.

What Poplawski didn't know was that Jauch saw Poplawski exclusively as someone who could challenge Bernie Ruoff for the kicker's job. He had no plans to use Poplawski as a receiver, and when Joe arrived in training camp, he wasn't even given an offensive playbook. The first couple of days he was consigned to the corner of the practice field where he and Ruoff kicked while the "real" players practised. On day three, the always polite and softspoken Poplawski worked up the courage to tell Jauch "I'd really like the opportunity to show what I can do as a receiver." Jauch consented and Joe spent that night memorizing the offensive playbook. The next day, Joe knew the plays better than all the rookies and some of the veterans. Jauch was suitably impressed, and one of the great receiving careers in CFL history was born.

Poplawski was named CFL rookie of the year in 1978. Twice he was named Top Canadian Player in the Schenley awards and on three other occasions he was the runner-up. Five times he was named an All-Canadian. He caught 549 passes for 8,341 yards over the nine years he played. We are all left to wonder how much more Poplawski would have achieved had he not retired at the age of 29. After the 1986 season, in which he won his second Schenley as best Canadian player, Poplawski started having trouble with his back. He also had trouble negotiating with Cal Murphy, who had taken over as General Manager in the wake of Paul Robson's departure to Ottawa. After a few days of sparring with Murphy, Poplawski decided it was time to get on with his after-football life. He had become very involved with Ranger Insurance and following one particularly unproductive discussion with Murphy, Joe said "Cal, I'm going to retire." And that was it. Murphy never got back to him and Poplawski formalized his retirement. Joe admits he had some second thoughts about quitting during that 1987 season, especially because the Bombers had a good team that had a chance to go all the way. Murphy asked him early in 1988 if he was interested in a comeback. By that time Poplawski's back problem had worsened, he had immersed himself in the insurance business and he closed the book completely on his playing career.

■ **'Joe Pop':** *Perennial CFL award winner.*

Winnipeg Free Press

No Bomber player in the 1970s and 80s, and I would suggest no receiver in Bomber history, caught it across the middle the way Joe Poplawski did. He is in the Winnipeg Football Club Hall of Fame and the Canadian Football Hall of Fame. And the Winnipeg community is richer for having Joe, wife Darlene, and sons Derek, Wade and Brent Poplawski as residents.

Bob Irving is sports director of CJOB 68 Radio.

BIG GAME FOOTBALL: THE TOP FOUR

BY DON WITTMAN

■ All-star Running back Dave Raimey and young fan: *'Can I have your chin-strap Mr. Raimey'?*

An almost half a century of watching the Winnipeg Blue Bombers, I have been witness to some games that will remain forever etched in my memory. Four of them truly stand out.

I covered my first ever Grey Cup game in 1961 and for a first trip to the national championship it was an unforgettable experience. Not only because it was a great game but it was the first and still the only Grey Cup game to be decided in overtime. The game was played December 2nd at Exhibition Stadium in Toronto, a crowd of 32,652 witnessed it, and Blue Bomber quarterback Ken Ploen scored the game winning touchdown in overtime as the Bombers beat the Hamilton Tiger-Cats 21-14.

The Bombers were back in Toronto the following year, again facing the Tiger-Cats in what almost seemed to be an autumn ritual. It was the fifth time in six seasons that Winnipeg and Hamilton had played in the Grey Cup. And that 1962 game became the first and only Grey Cup game that required two days to determine a winner. CNE stadium was often subjected to some nasty weather conditions because of its proximity to Lake Ontario. On that first day of December a heavy blanket of fog began rolling in off the lake and by early in the fourth quarter not only was it virtually impossible for the television cameras and the fans to follow the play, visibility was also a problem for the two teams. As a result, commissioner G. Sydney Halter suspended play with 9:29 remaining in the fourth quarter and the Bombers leading 28-27. He ordered the balance of the game to be played the next day. In the only two-day Grey Cup game in history, the Bombers were able to protect their one point advantage and win their fourth Grey Cup in five seasons.

The 1965 Grey Cup game, again at CNE stadium and again featuring Winnipeg and Hamilton, will be remembered for the howling winds that blew in off the lake. The game set a record for conceded safety touches as the Bombers, when deep in their own territory and forced to punt, would give up two points rather than attempt a kick that would barely make it past the line of scrimmage. Those three safety touches proved to be the difference as Hamilton won the "Wind Bowl" 22-16, handing Bud Grant his first Grey Cup defeat after four victories.

The unique rules of Canadian football also produced one of the wildest finishes ever to a playoff game. The year was 1972, the scene the Western final at Winnipeg Stadium. Winnipeg and Saskatchewan were tied at 24 with just seconds remaining. Saskatchewan's Jack Abendschan attempted a field goal that would give the green and white the victory and a trip to the Grey Cup. Even a miss and single point would be good enough for the win. In anticipation that the kick could be wide the Bombers sent three receivers into the end zone. Abendschan's kick was wide and the Bombers promptly punted the ball out of the end zone. But the Riders' Ron Lancaster kicked it right back in. Again the Bombers recovered, kicked it back out, and it looked like the game might go to overtime. Amidst all the confusion with players on both sides scrambling for the ball, Winnipeg was called for no yards. Saskatchewan thus retained possession. This time Abendschan's field goal attempt split the uprights and the Roughriders were bound for the Grey Cup while Winnipeg fans left the stadium shocked and disappointed.

Of the many, many Blue Bomber games I've seen and the many great Bomber memories I have, those four games are the ones that I remember most vividly.

Don Wittman is a veteran CBC sports announ

A NEW GM AND A NEW COACH

Robson tried his best to convince Johnny Michels, who had served so ably for so many years as Bud Grant's chief assistant, to leave the Minnesota Vikings and return to Winnipeg as head coach of the Bombers. When Michels said no, Robson turned to his second choice, and what a stroke of brilliance it turned out to be. Early in 1983, Robson introduced Cal Murphy as the Bombers 18th head coach. Murphy had compiled a long and impressive CFL coaching resume that started with B.C. in 1976 and carried on to include six consecutive Grey Cup victories as an assistant coach, five in Edmonton and one in Montreal. He also brought an Irish fire and determination that was never to be underestimated.

Bomber Hall of Fame offensive lineman Chris Walby said Murphy had two particular attributes that made him successful. "Cal recognized talent like no one else, and he never let players get complacent, instilling a fear so that you never for a minute thought your job was safe regardless of your status on the team." Murphy also surrounded himself with good people. His first player personnel director was Bill Polian, who went on to fame and fortune in the NFL. Polian's replacement, Paul Jones, would find some of the top players in club history.

■ **All-world receiver**
James Murphy: ***His glue fingers in the 1984 West final propelled the Bombers to the Grey Cup.***

Murphy inherited a solid football team from Ray Jauch, and he started the 1983 season with an infusion of new players that included Jeff Boyd, James Murphy, Ken Hailey, David Shaw, John Hufnagel, Tyrone Jones, Willard Reaves and Sean Kehoe. Murphy also inherited a quarterback controversy. Dieter Brock had been named the CFL's Most Outstanding player in both 1980 and 1981. After he turned in another stellar performance during the 1982 season, Brock and his agent, Gil Scott, decided that the "Birmingham Rifle," as Brock had come to be known, was underpaid. As often happens in these situations, a massive difference of opinion developed between the general manager, Robson, and the player, Brock, over his precise worth.

What developed was the most highly publicized and longest-running contract dispute in club history. Brock was a training camp holdout and didn't report until the night before the first game. Murphy started Nickie Hall in the first two

SEAN SALISBURY: THE 'SALISBURY NIP'

BY JIM BENDER

Sean Salisbury authored one of the briefest but most interesting football chapters of the decade in 1988-89.

During the winter of 1988, the Blue Bombers had lost quarterback Tom Clements to retirement and the pursuit of a replacement began. General Manager Cal Murphy lured veteran B.C. quarterback Roy Dewalt to Winnipeg but he spent the season nursing tendonitis. Murphy finally settled on Tom Muecke, who had been the backup to Clements, as his starter but kept on looking at other possibilities. One of those was Sean Salisbury.

The U.S.C. grad became an instant hero here once he got his chance—something that was to be quickly forgotten just a season later. But the 6-foot-5, 210-pound pivot turned the struggling Bombers around. He completed 100 of 202 passes for 1,556 yards and 11 touchdowns, with five interceptions, in seven appearances. And Salisbury looked like the quarterback of the future that the Bombers had been seeking as he led them into the CFL playoffs by winning four of the six games he started. Not only that but he won fans over with his 'Aw-shucks' attitude and down-home charm.

While Salisbury was performing those heroics, the Bombers dealt Dewalt to Ottawa, tying their fortunes to Salisbury's gun. And he did not disappoint. Salisbury completed 25 of 40 passes for 332 yards and two TDs to lead Winnipeg to a 35-28 victory over Hamilton in the Eastern Semifinal. He followed that up with a shakier 18-of-34 for 223 yards and no touchdowns as the Bombers upset Toronto 27-11 in the Eastern Final. But suddenly, Salisbury et al were Grey Cup-bound.

Although Salisbury completed only 12 of 32 passes for 246 yards on a blustery day in Ottawa and the Winnipeg offence was held to just 18 yards in the second half, the Bombers still managed to beat the B.C. Lions 22-21 to capture Cup glory.

But that Cup euphoria may have gone to Salisbury's head as he demanded a new, multi-year pact. He first agreed to terms, then declined, which caused a rift between himself and GM Cal Murphy. In fact, Salsibury's agent, John Boggs, called Murphy's offer "embarrassing." Murphy said Salisbury "basically called me an ingrate," according to Winnipeg newspapers.

Salisbury eventually agreed to play but did not have a banner year in 1989, completing less than 50 percent of his passes in 17 games. The defending Grey Cup champs limped to a 7-11 record, still good enough for third place. But the biggest shocker of all came when Murphy decided that he had had enough of Salisbury on the eve of the playoffs. The deciding factor was an article that appeared in an L.A. newspaper that quoted Salisbury saying, among other things, how much he hated playing in deal Winnipeg. Some interpreted that to mean that the native Californian hated Canada and could not wait to

■ Grey Cup winner Sean Salisbury: *Good arm and playmaking ability.*

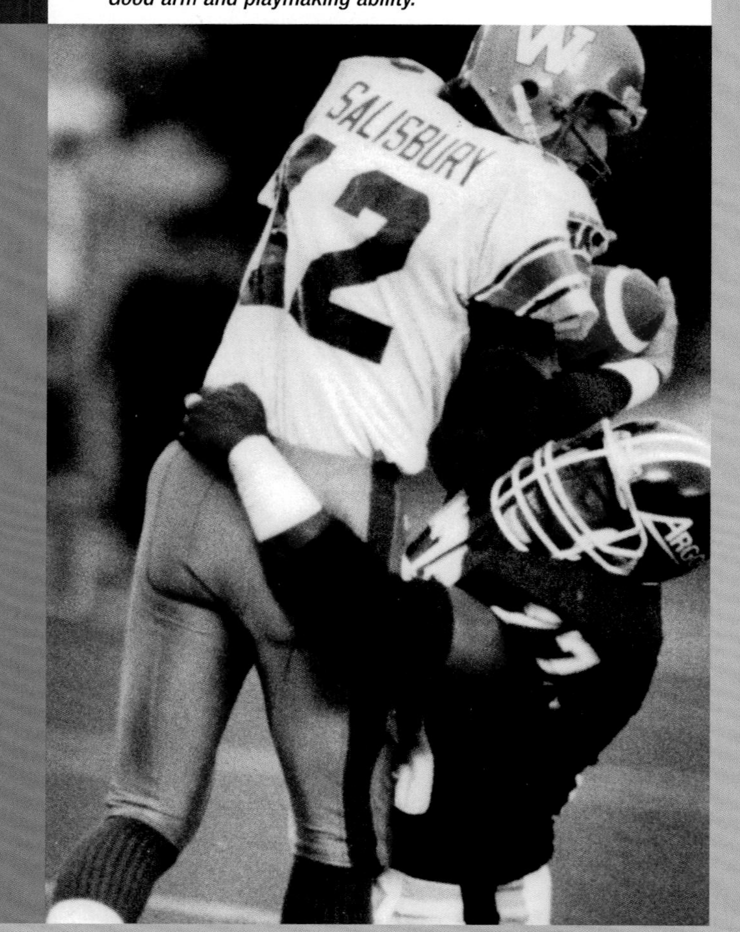

Winnipeg Free Press

■ Quarterback Sean Salisbury: *Didn't see eye to eye with GM Cal Murphy.*

jump to the NFL. So, Murphy let him go. But several Bombers privately questioned the timing of the move.

When he was released, a disappointed Salisbury said that he would always have that Grey Cup victory on his resume. Murphy would later say that Winnipeg basically won the 1988 Cup without a quarterback.

And so, that little nip in Bomber history that started with a Grey Cup bang ended quickly with a Salisbury whimper.

Jim Bender is a football writer with the Winnipeg Sun.

games, but, understanding that a football coach's meal ticket is always the quarterback, Murphy was only too happy to insert Brock in the second game when Hall got hurt. Brock led the Bombers to four straight wins before staging another walkout. He returned two days before the next game, August 20th in B.C. Place. Poorly prepared, Brock threw five interceptions in a 44-6 loss and got pulled for the first time in his career.

After that game, a highly agitated Robson held a memorable "state of the union" press conference in which he firmly decried Brock's tactics, stated that the football club would not be held hostage by their quarterback and suspended Brock without pay. This prompted the famous Brock quote in which the quarterback said "How many times can you go to the zoo?" The acrimony between Brock and Robson had reached a breaking point and in a stroke of genius, or luck, or perhaps both, Robson and Murphy found a team that coveted Brock. That team was also anxious to get rid of their quarterback, who had become immensely unpopular with the local fans. On September 21st, 1983, the Blue Bombers traded Brock to Hamilton, straight-up for Tom Clements.

The Bombers finished that tumultuous first year of Murphy's rule at 9-7 losing the western final to the Lions 39-21 But Murphy knew he had found a quarterback who was a winner, and while Dieter Brock left behind a hall-of-fame legacy, the best of the Murphy-era was just about to begin.

The Bombers began the 1984 season with Clements and John Hufnagel as their quarterbacks. They had

Winnipeg Free Press

SHORT YARDAGE

Did you know: During 'blow outs' in the 1980s, when the Bombers were well ahead near the end of the game, the receivers would play 'rock, paper, scissors' to see who would play the last few plays of the game.

found a stud running back named Willard Reaves, who was coming off a sensational rookie season. Fullback Pat Cantner led the blocking for Reaves. James Murphy and Jeff Boyd had also arrived in '83 to join Joe Poplawski and Rick House in the receiving corps along with local product Kevin Neiles. Chris Walby had come into his own as the best offensive lineman in the CFL and he had all-Canadians John Bonk and Nick Bastaja lining up next to him. Homegrown products Doug MacIver and Stan Mikawos joined Tony Norman on a solid defensive line, Aaron Brown and Tyrone Jones led a menacing linebacking corps, Ken Hailey, Scott Flagel and David Shaw were the heart of a strong secondary, Vernon Pahl was the special teams ace and Trevor Kennerd and Bob Cameron provided stellar kicking. The Eskimos had started to decline after their run of five straight Grey Cup wins, and the Bombers were confident they could give a powerful B.C. Lions team coached by Don Mathews, a vigorous argument for the West Division title. What followed was one of the more memorable seasons in Bomber history.

The team lost its opener and then rolled up seven wins in a row. With an explosive offence, that produced a league-high 523 points, and a stingy defence that allowed just 309, the Bombers went 11-4-1. Problem was, they lost their regular season finale 20-3 in B.C., to finish second behind the 12-3-1 Lions. If the long Grey Cup drought was going to end, it would have to include a win on the road in the very unfriendly confines of B.C. Place Stadium. The Bombers easily took care of the first order of post-season business, crushing the fading Eskimos 55-20 in a semi-final game at sold-out Winnipeg Stadium.

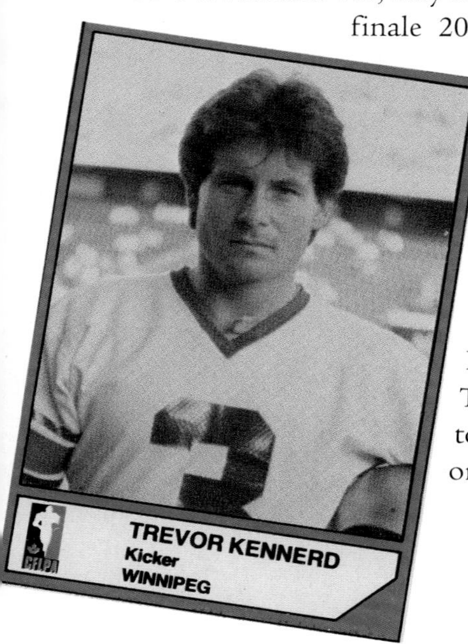

Now came the hard part, a trip to Vancouver and a showdown with a very good B.C. team that had become practically unbeatable at home since they opened their domed stadium, B.C. Place, in 1982. Fans turned out 60,000 strong in support of their Leos, and the noise that reverberated off the white canvas roof that covered the dome provided the Lions with a "13th" man that few teams had an answer for. But Cal Murphy and his team were ready. Using earplugs and hand signals on offence, the Bombers walked into B.C. Place and stunned the Lions 31-14. Clements had a fabulous game, as

Winnipeg Free Press

■ **CFL award winner Paul Bennett returning a punt vs Montréal:** ***Hard-nosed, he didn't like to run out of bounds.***

■ Tom Clements: *A quarterback who could beat you with his arm, his feet or his brain.*

did Reaves. James Murphy made a catch for a touchdown that is still considered one of the best in CFL history. And Winnipeg's defence had B.C. quarterback Roy Dewalt on the run all day.

Blue Bomber General Manager Paul Robson was so emotional after the game that he had to compose himself on a couple of occasions before he could speak to the media. And when they arrived back in Winnipeg, the scene was almost indescribable as total bedlam engulfed Winnipeg Airport. Thousands of fans tried to cram into the terminal. As Murphy recalled, "I remember Paul Robson telling me to put my hands on his shoulders and don't stop moving. I've never seen anything like it." The monumental victory in Vancouver kicked off a week of celebrating the likes of which hadn't been seen for at least two decades. Robson, Murphy and the players savoured every minute of it, without losing sight of the fact they still had one mountain to climb before their journey was complete.

FINALLY, THE CUP RETURNS

The 1984 Grey Cup game was historic in that it was the first to ever be held in Edmonton. The Bombers had a powerhouse team, while the Hamilton Tiger Cats had gone 6-9-1 before clawing their way out of an embarassingly weak Eastern Division, upsetting Toronto 14-13 in an overtime East final. The story line was Clements against Brock, and although no one knew it at the time, Clements had suffered a punctured lung in the West final. It was common knowledge Clements was injured but the Bombers kept the details a secret. Clements received medical clearance to play, and the Clements-Brock showdown was on. Whether it was stage fright, or frost bite is open to debate, but the Bombers got off to a horrible start as 60,081 fans huddled up in parkas and snowmobile gear at Commonwealth stadium watched the Tiger Cats jump out to a 14-0 lead. A Bernie Ruoff field goal early in the 2nd quarter gave Hamilton a 17-3 edge and a major

upset was in the making. That's when the high-powered Bombers exploded. Clements, who had left the game in favour of John Hufnagel because of a contact lense problem, returned to the field and the Bombers caught fire. Willard Reaves scored on a 3-yard run, Stan Mikawos recovered a fumble and returned it 22 yards for a touchdown, Clements found Poplawski with a 12-yard scoring pass and Trevor Kennerd added three converts and two field goals to cap a 27 point Blue Bomber eruption, which was a Grey Cup record for points in one quarter.

Hamilton never scored again, the Bombers added 17 second-half points, and the final score was a resounding 47-17. Clements was named the game's outstanding player. His three game post-

■ **(Above, from left) James Murphy, Jeff Boyd, Willard Reaves with Grey Cup, 1984:** ***'We are the champions, my friend.'***

■ **1984 Grey Cup ring:** ***The first 'bling' since 1962, ending a 22-year drought.***

season total was 61 completions out of 86 passes for 933 yards and eight touchdowns. Canadian running back Sean Kehoe, an Edmonton native, emerged as an unlikely Grey Cup hero. He rushed for 89 yards, which was 35 yards more than his entire season total, and caught five passes for 47 yards to earn Canadian player of the game honours. Linebacker Tyrone Jones was named the defensive star of the game, and the Bombers 22-year Grey Cup drought was over. Those of us who were in the Bomber locker room will never forget club president Jan Brown hoisting the Grey Cup, then passing it around as tears of joy filled a champion's dressing room that was normally inhabited by the Eskimos.

Bomber fans went wild. When the team returned home from Edmonton they staged a Grey Cup victory party in the Winnipeg Arena. 15,000 fans nearly lifted the roof off the home of the Jets during player introductions, and Paul Robson uttered his famous line to Winnipeggers: "When it's 30 below in the middle of January and your car won't start, this Grey Cup victory means we'll all feel a little warmer."

Paul Robson decided it was time for new challenges and shocked the Winnipeg football community by resigning as Bomber GM to become the general manager of the Ottawa Rough Riders.

Getting to the top is one thing, staying there is quite another. Winning the West during the '80s was a major challenge. The Bombers went 12-4 during their Grey Cup encore year, only to watch the Lions post a 13-3 record. The Bombers handled Edmonton 22-15 in a hard-fought semi-final but this time they couldn't solve the riddle of B.C. Place as the Lions crushed the Bombers 42-22 in the West Final. In 1986, with Clements and most of the core of the 1984 team still intact, The Bombers led the CFL in scoring for the third year in a row. Among their successes was a 56-0 win over Saskatchewan. They finished a very respectable 11-7, which was only good enough for third in the West behind Edmonton and B.C.. Once again B.C.

MY FAVOURITE TEAM: THE 1988 BOMBERS

BY JOE PASCUCCI

I was just ten when my cousin took me to my first Canadian Football League game, October 8th, 1967. It was at CNE Stadium in Toronto. The Argonauts were playing the Blue Bombers that day. While I can't recall any particular play from the game, I've never forgotten the final score. It was 53 to 0 and it wasn't for the Bombers.

When I moved to Winnipeg from Toronto in January 1982, the Bombers were on the verge of their first Grey Cup since the Bud Grant era in 1962. In 1984 the Bombers finally ended 22 years of frustration with a blowout Grey Cup win over the Tiger-Cats. There would be two more Grey Cup celebrations in the next six years for the Bombers.

It was, however, the unexpected victory by the Bombers in 1988 that I remember best. 1988 was a transition year for the CFL and the Bombers. Gone was the league's fat television contract. Community-run organizations like the Bombers faced a new economic reality. Especially when it came to players' salaries.

Rather than accept a huge pay cut, quarterback Tom Clements, the CFL's outstanding player in 1987, retired to begin work as a lawyer. Running back Willard Reaves and wide receiver Jeff Boyd were asked to accept less. Both refused and were ultimately released. Boyd ended up with the Argos; Reaves went to the NFL. Meanwhile linebacker Tyrone Jones had played out his option year to give the NFL a shot.

So when it was time to start the regular season the Bombers weren't anyone's choice to win the Grey Cup. This was Mike Riley's second season as head coach and he was under pressure after a disappointing conclusion to the season in 1987.

The season began with Roy Dewalt at quarterback. Dewalt had taken the B.C. Lions to a Grey Cup championship in 1985. But with the Bombers Dewalt quickly showed that he no longer had the throwing arm to be effective.

Tom Muecke, in his third season, came off the bench to lead the Bombers to memorable last minute wins over Calgary and then Saskatchewan, resulting in the release of Dewalt. But by September Muecke was again the backup; this time to Sean Salisbury.

Offensively the Bombers were barely adequate that year. They ranked near the bottom in most offensive categories. Murphy, the CFL's outstanding player in 1986, was the exception, with over 1,400 yards and 10 touchdowns.

Defensively the Bombers could hold their own. Up front there was Michael Gray and Stan Mikowas. Heading up the linebacking corps were James West, Greg Battle and Aaron Brown, the undisputed defensive leader of the Bombers' Grey Cup winning team in '84. The secondary featured Ken Hailey, Ken Pettway, and Darryl Sampson, James Jefferson, Rod Hill, and Bennie Thompson. Veterans Bob Cameron and Trevor Kennerd handled the kicking duties.

But what this Bomber team had, and what made them my favourite team was a solid supporting cast. No CFL team wins without good Canadians and the Bombers of 1988 had the likes of Vernon Pahl, Tony Johns, Dan Wicklum, Michael Allen, Paul Clatney, Paul Shorten, Leon Hatziioannou, and Randy Fabi. Though their time on the field was limited, they were as important to that Grey Cup-winning season as players like Murphy and Hill. The Bombers weren't good enough to win unless everyone did their part on game day.

Despite the constant lineup shuffling, the Bombers were a respectable 9 and 6 and challenging for first in the East until back to back losses to the Argos late in the season put an end to that. Those defeats were part of a three-game losing streak for the Bombers as they closed out the regular season with a 9 and 9 record. Because they were in the Eastern Conference that was good enough for a second place finish and a home playoff game against the Tiger Cats.

However, the majority of fans had written off the team and the year. That's why only 12,210 bothered to brave the cold to show up for the Eastern semifinal. In the game the Bombers would lose both Chris Walby and Greg Battle through injuries. Yet they would prevail 35-28 over the Ti-Cats with perhaps the biggest play of the season: Scott Flagel accidentally tripping up Earl Winfield on his way into the end zone on a punt return. Hamilton settled for a field goal and the Bombers scored a touchdown on their next possession and never looked back. In fact the Bombers seem to come together as a team for the first time that season. They were suddenly a confident group as the Argos would find that out the following weekend in the Eastern Final.

It really came together for this unlikely team in the Grey Game game against the B.C. Lions. Offensively, Murphy was unstoppable in the first half with five receptions for 165 yards and a touchdown. Defensively, the Bombers bent a little bit in the first 30 minutes but were rock solid in the second half. They stuffed Matt Dunigan on third and one, and Hill and Gray would make memorable interceptions. Gray's game-saver was forever know by Bomber fans as the "immaculate interception."

Special teams made their contributions too. Blocking a Lui Passaglia field goal attempt here, forcing a fumble there. Suddenly Trevor Kennerd was in position to kick the winning field goal. Which he calmly did.

However the best performance of the day might have been that of Bob Cameron. It was Cameron's ability to punt the ball into a stiff wind that made the difference. He provided the luxury of good field position throughout the game.

It was a victory in which each Bomber player on the field could truthfully say they contributed. I won't forget a second of their incredible playoff performance and the transformation of 37 players into Grey Cup champions. They are my favourite team.

Joe Pascucci is sports director at Global TV, Winnipeg.

Winnipeg Free Press

■ **Head Coach Mike Riley:** ***Honest and true with a great football mind, he had the players' respect.***

■ **(Below) 1988 Blue Bombers:** ***Getting hot in the playoffs all the way to the Cup.***

Stan Mikawos and Quincy Williams celebrate QB sack. *Defence wins championships.*

Winnipeg Free Pr

SHORT YARDAGE

Did you know: Cigarette smoking cornerback David Shaw, stepped in front of a pass at his own five yard line and was taking it back the other way for what appeared to be an easy touchdown when he ran out of gas and was tackled by Ottawa's Nick Benjamin just before he crossed the goal line. Benjamin was a 290 pound offensive lineman!

Place was their undoing, they lost a tough 21-14 semi-final game, and the dynasty dreams were over. Cal Murphy said later that one of his great disappointments was that those '85 and '86 teams didn't get to the Cup.

The 1987 season would bring dramatic change to the CFL and to the Bombers hierarchy. Paul Robson decided it was time for new challenges and shocked the Winnipeg football community by resigning as Bomber GM to become the general manager of the Ottawa Rough Riders. Robson was wooed by money and what he referred to as "the middle-age crazies." Cal Murphy argued aggressively that he could handle both the coach and GM portfolios but it was one of the few debates he lost in his Blue Bomber tenure. Former club president Jan Brown and other members of the teams executive were adamant that Murphy choose only one role. Cal Murphy reluctantly opted for the manager's chair and began the search for someone to replace him as head coach.

RILEY, THE SEQUEL

Former Edmonton quarterback Bruce Lemmerman, who had played on three Edmonton Grey Cup winners and coached on two others, was considered a favourite to take over. Murphy, however, had other ideas. After a series of meetings with the man he wanted, including one at the Minneapolis airport where Murphy had to convince this individual he was ready to be a head coach in the CFL, Murphy introduced his replacement at a packed news conference in the Blue and Gold Room. When Mike Riley strolled out of the Blue and Gold kitchen, you could hear a pin drop. It didn't take long for the room to burst

Winnipeg Blue Bombers

■ (From left) Premier Howard Pawley, General Manager Paul Robson, Mayor Bill Norrie: '*Welcome to Winnerpeg.*'

into applause. Riley, son of Bud, had been a very popular assistant coach under Murphy before leaving for a job at Northern Colorado in 1986. He was intelligent, classy, and quickly proved that he was more than capable of being a CFL head coach despite his tender age of thirty-three. What Riley didn't know, when he took the job, was that he would be leading the Blue Bombers into the CFL's Eastern Division. Just prior to the start of the '87 season, the Montreal Concordes folded leaving only three teams in the East. To create two four-team divisions, the CFL moved the Bombers into the East with Toronto, Hamilton and Ottawa. This didn't necessarily sit well with Bomber fans. Winnipeg sees itself as a western Canadian city. Any connection with the

SHORT YARDAGE

Did you know: Blue Bomber all-star defensive end Pete Catan loved to amuse his teammates during practises by firing rockets off of his helmet. These rockets would travel upwards of 1,000 feet into the air... some going over the east-side stands and almost hitting the Polo Park Inn.

East is viewed as coincidence and not necessarily palatable.

The upside of the move was that the CFL East was littered with weak teams, and the Bombers figured to have things very much their way. Which was exactly the case. Riley's first year as head coach saw the Bombers score a club record 554 points and roll up a 12-6 record that earned them a first place finish, one point ahead of the Toronto Argonauts. Only one problem. The Argos were pretty good. Led by running back Gill Fenerty and a solid defence anchored by Willie Pless and Rodney Harding, the Argos walked into Winnipeg and stunned the Blue Bombers 19-3 in the East Final. The frustration of once again coming up short in an effort to win another Grey Cup stung deeply through the Winnipeg football community and the team which still featured a core of stars including Clements, Reaves, Mikawos, Walby, Bastaja, Hailey, Murphy, Jeff Boyd, Perry Tuttle, Lyle Bauer, Dave Black, Bob Molle, Ty Jones, James West, Scott Flagel, Darryl Sampson, James Jefferson, Roy Bennett, Delbert Fowler, Bob Cameron, Trevor Kennerd and a rookie named Greg Battle.

1988 produced more challenges for Mike Riley. Much to everyone's surprise, Tom Clements decided in April that his contract wasn't to his liking and he was going to retire to make use of his lawyer's degree. That left the Bombers short at the quarterback position with training camp only six weeks away. Murphy pursued David Archer and Roy Dewalt. He wound up with DeWalt, who had been cut loose by the B.C. Lions after eight productive years on the West Coast. It didn't take long to see why the Lions had decided Dewalt was finished. His arm was shot and the Bombers eventually shipped Dewalt to Ottawa in exchange for defensive lineman Leon Hatziioannou.

Dewalt's struggles gave third year backup quarterback Tom Muecke a chance to show what he could do. Muecke performed adequately, but Murphy and Riley knew they still had to upgrade the position, and in September, they signed Sean Salisbury, who was ready to try the CFL after three years of failing to breakinto the NFL. Murphy was ecstatic. He believed he had secured the solution to the Bombers quarterbacking dilemma. Salisbury was a product of the University of Southern California. He came

■ **The lovely and talented Blue Brigade, 1987:** ***Working as hard as the football players to entertain the fans.***

Winnipeg Free Press

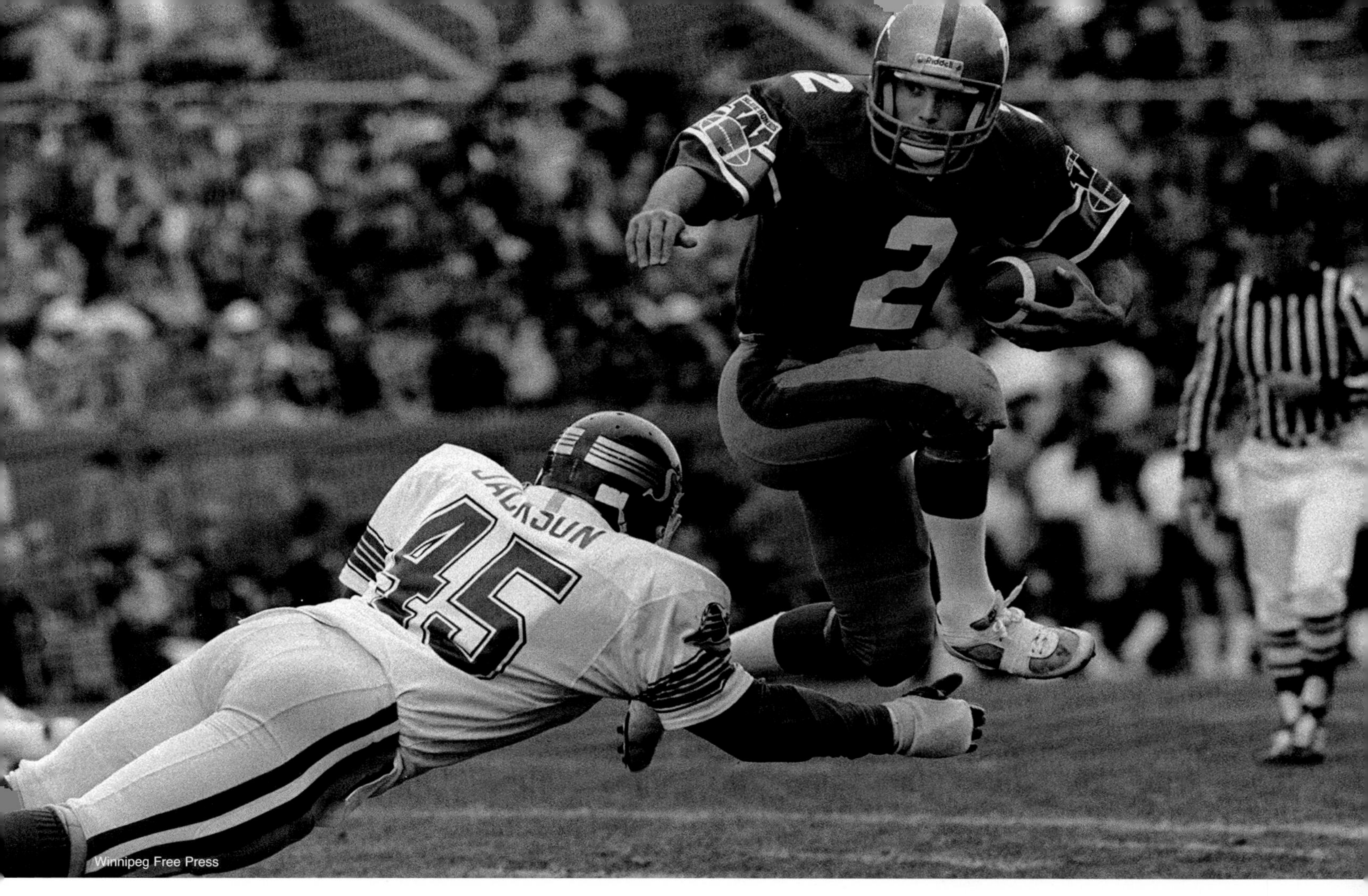

■ CFL All-star QB Tom Clements: *Now you see me… now you don't.*

to Winnipeg with size, 6'5", a big arm and a big ego disguised as an engaging personality. He quickly took over the starting spot, threw for 11 touchdowns and only five interceptions, and gave the Bombers hope despite a mediocre 9-9 third place finish.

Salisbury directed the Bombers to a 35-28 semi-final win over Hamilton at snow-covered Winnipeg Stadium, and then led them to a 27-11 upset win over the 14-4 Argos in the East Final. Salisbury was the toast of the town as the Bombers headed off to the Grey Cup in Ottawa to meet Matt Dunigan and the B.C. Lions, who had scored upset wins in Saskatchewan and Edmonton en route to a date with the Bombers. It was a gorgeous 14 degrees Celsius on November 28th in Ottawa, but the wind was howling and it turned into a game of turnovers, big plays and field position. Bob Cameron enhanced his reputation as the best wind-kicker the CFL has ever seen, coming up with one of the greatest punting displays in Grey Cup history. Cameron averaged a staggering 47.6 yards on 12 kicks, repeatedly pinning the Lions deep in their own end. Placekicker Trevor Kennerd added four field goals and a single duplicating the super kicking display he had put on in the 1984 Grey Cup.

Salisbury only completed 12 of 32 passes but they covered 246 yards, and he found James Murphy for a 35-yard touchdown strike that tied the game at 14-14 in the second quarter. Murphy had a monster game, catching five passes for 165 yards. The game swayed back and forth. With 58 seconds remaining and the Bombers clinging to a 22-19 lead, Dunigan put together what had all the appearance of a game-winning drive until Bomber defensive end Michael Gray made the "immaculate interception." James West tipped a Dunigan pass deep in Bomber territory into Gray's waiting arms, and the Bombers had their long-awaited second Grey Cup Championship of the 80s.

■ Safety Scott Flagel breaks up a pass vs Calgary with help from DB Ken Hailey: *Don't come around here no more.*

The Bombers opened the 1989 season fully expecting to contend again. Salisbury and Murphy had reached an uneasy truce over the quaterback's unresolved contract dispute. With Salisbury at the controls, and Walby, Bauer, Black, Murphy, Tuttle, Gray, West, Battle, Sampson, House, Tim Jessie, Paul Randolph, Rod Hill, Ken Hailey and others back from the 1988 championship team, the prospects of a third title in the decade were bright.

...the 1970s and 80s produced some of the greatest triumphs, the most engaging and colourful characters and some of the finest players that have donned a Bomber uniform.

Back-to-back September wins against B.C. left the Bombers with a 7-4 record. Little did anyone know how dramatically it would all come unravelled. Close losses at home to Hamilton and Toronto started the decline. Salisbury threw 11 interceptions during a 5-game losing streak and as the pressure built, he became what Murphy called a "disruptive and divisive force with his finger-pointing." Salisbury refused to take what Murphy and Riley felt was his share of the blame, and when the Bombers dropped their sixth in a row at home against Ottawa, Riley told Murphy that he had to cut Salisbury.

Murphy gave the move his full blessing as a season of promise had turned into a chaos-riddled soap opera. Salisbury's departure cleared the poisoned air around the club. Lee Saltz took over at quarterback with Sam Garza as his backup, and even though the Bombers lost their final regular season game to finish the year with seven straight losses and a 7-11 record, the players were optimistic they could pull some surprises in the playoffs. And they did. With Saltz performing solidly, the Bombers, for the second year in a row, walked into Toronto and shocked the Argos in the East Final. This time the score was 30-7, Saltz passed for 178 yards and two touchdowns, rushed for another 87.

■ Willard Reaves: *Like many Bombers he elected to stay in the community and now works as a sheriff with the provincial prison system.*

The Bombers headed off to Hamilton for the East Final convinced they could give the 12-6 Tiger Cats all they wanted. They did. Saltz passed for 308 yards, including an 87-yard touchdown to House. Had Trevor Kennerd not missed two makeable field goals, with a third being blocked, the Bombers might have miraculously transformed a 7-11 season into a Grey Cup appearance. As it was, Hamilton prevailed 14-10 and one of the most chaotic seasons in Bomber history was over.

So, the Bombers ended the decade of the '80s on a downer. But the 1970s and '80s produced some of the greatest triumphs, the most engaging and colourful characters and some of the finest players that have donned a Bomber uniform. They were largely times to remember fondly. From Bud Riley to Ray Jauch, Cal Murphy to Mike Riley, Bomber fans were treated to mostly winning, exciting football. Many of the Bombers all-time great players surfaced during this 20-year period Brock, Clements, Walby, Poplawski, Murphy, Reaves, Helton, Hill, Bennett, Holmes, House, Washington, Battle, Jones, West, Kennerd, Cameron, Tuttle, Mikawos, Frank and Bauer went on to have Hall-of-Fame careers. ■

SHORT YARDAGE

Did you know: One day after practice veteran centre John Bonk didn't like the crowded cold tub in the training room and proceeded to clear the tub by discovering an 'O-Henry' bar floating around. He then pulled a 'Bill Murray' and ate the bar.

■ Greg Battle, Michael Gray, Quincy Williams gang-tackle Eskimo running back: *Bombers boasted the best defence in the CFL in 1990.*

CHAPTER 4

1990-2005

A BUMPY RIDE

BY ED TAIT

Please fasten your seat belts and insure that your tray tables are in the upright and secured position. Yes, buckle up Bomber fans, as we are going to take you on a retrospective journey through some of the most turbulent times in the club's storied 75 years.

Among many stops, we'll revisit the team's last Grey Cup title—some 15 years ago now, the heartache of three championship failures since and the franchise identity crisis caused by five division changes—from East to North to West to East to West, all since 1990.

We'll witness the resiliency of the community-owned organization, from surviving its own desperate cash calls over the last 15 years and the unmitigated disaster that was the U.S. expansion experiment to the near-death and subsequent rebirth of the Canadian Football League itself. There will be the touching story of a legendary

Winnipeg Free Press

■ **Running back Robert Mimbs:** ***High-stepping it for the first down against Toronto.***

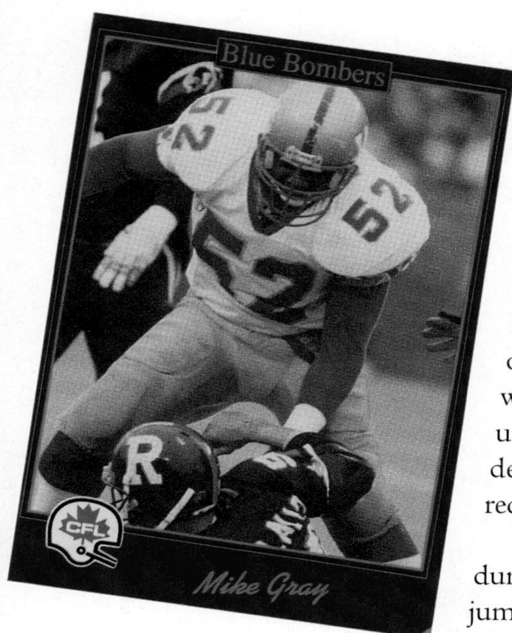

coach who was miraculously saved on the operating table while waiting for a new heart. And there will be tall tales of the man who replaced him—a complete antithesis of the coaching stereotype who somehow enjoyed unprecedented popularity despite a grotesque 6-26 record.

Finally, we'll touch down during an era in which the team jumped off the gurney and raced from the intensive care unit back to good health courtesy an old-school coach and his talent-sleuth sidekick, a likeable quarterback snatched from the bottom of the B.C. Lions depth chart and the return of a Bomber Hall-of-Fame centre who straight-armed the creditors and helped steer the whole operation away from rocky shores.

So settle in for the ride, folks. There will be clear, sunny skies and spectacular views that will leave you positively breathless.... And we'll relive choppy sequences of Bomber seasons past that will have you reaching for the air-sickness bag.

But as has always been the case in the team's long history, the journey certainly won't have you snoozing in your seat...

THE LAST TITLE

We begin in 1990 when, just as they are now, the on-field Bombers were a difficult bunch to read.

Remember, the '88 Grey Cup team was hardly dominant and the '89 edition finished an uninspiring 7-11 before losing to Hamilton in the East Division Final.

And so the key issue for the Bombers as a new decade broke was the iffy state of their quarterbacking. In the years following the exit of all-star Tom Clements the club would trot out the likes of Roy Dewalt, Tom Muecke, Sean Salisbury and Lee Saltz in what seemed like an ongoing audition for any pivot who could consistently run an efficient offence while the dominant, ball-hawking defensive dozen that was the team's backbone wreaked havoc across the land.

But with the unproven Saltz and Sam Garza listed as 1-2 on the depth chart, the Bombers entered training camp in '90 picked by most pundits to finish last in the division and considered nothing but extreme long shots to be slurping champagne from the Grey Cup come late November.

And while the Grey Cup looked to be a solid matchup on paper with the Bombers meeting Tracy Ham and the 10-8 Eskimos, there was zero hype all week and little drama even in the first part of the game.

Then on Canada Day—11 days before the opening of the season—Cal Murphy would make one of the shrewdest moves during his tenure by acquiring quarterback Tom Burgess from Saskatchewan for Saltz, the rights to receiver Allan Boyko and two first-round draft choices.

Burgess, who had split time with Kent Austin quarterbacking the Grey Cup champion Green Riders in '89, would often confound fans here in River City with his penchant for interceptions—he threw 56 vs. 52 touchdown passes in two years in Bomber colours—but he had two endearing qualities. First, he was absolutely adored by his teammates in the offensive huddle—Chris Walby still refers to him as the toughest QB with whom he's ever played—and he had a knack for coming up huge in the championship run of '90.

Still, the Bomber offence that season stunk with a capital 'S.' Winnipeg's offence finished dead last in scoring and was wounded badly with all-everything receiver James Murphy on the shelf for six games and the playoffs with a bum leg. But head coach Mike Riley knew that with his stingy 'Blue Thunder' defence that would set a CFL record with 48 interceptions, force 89 turnovers overall and give up 112 fewer points than any other team, the attack didn't need to make the scoreboard light up every week.

Instead, with running back Robert Mimbs grinding out a league-best 1,341 yards and the

John E. Sokolowski

defence doing its thing, with a sassy attitude that drove opponents berserk, the Bombers cruised to a surprising 12-6 regular-season record and first in the East Division.

That set the stage for the November dramatics of Burgess and the Bomber defence. The East Final, played at Winnipeg Stadium, featured the Argonauts who had an explosive offensive team that averaged 38 points per game and included the likes of receiver Darrell K. Smith, Matt Dunigan, Mike Clemons, Jeff Boyd and Paul Masotti. But even with Dunigan injured, the game wasn't decided until there were but a few ticks left on the clock. With the score tied at 17-17, Burgess—who often ran like he was dragging a refrigerator behind him—scrambled 31 yards to set up a 32-yard Trevor Kennerd game-winning field goal, his fourth of the day.

And while the Grey Cup looked to be a solid matchup on paper with the Bombers meeting Tracy Ham and the 10-8 Eskimos, there was zero hype all week and little drama even in the first part of the game.

Winnipeg would lead 10-4 at halftime and then iced the Eskimos with a 28-point third quarter—a Grey Cup scoring record that still stands—on a spectacular interception return by the CFL's top defender, Greg Battle, along with Burgess to Perry Tuttle and Warren Hudson TD strikes and a two-yard romp by Hudson.

Battle was superb, picking off two passes in being named the game's top defensive player while Hudson was the top Canadian. Burgess, who was good on 18 of 31 passes for 286 yards with three TDs against zero interceptions before being relieved by Danny McManus, was voted the top offensive star as the Bombers became the unlikeliest of champions.

"Nobody thought a lot of this team," said Riley afterward. "We were picked last and we finished first. The defence was on top of its game all season and it was really on top in this one."

"The thing I like about this team," added wide receiver Eric Streater, "is this has always been known as a team that played together. You don't

BEST OF THE BEST: GREY CUP FEVER

BY ED TAIT

Football fans love to debate, usually over a vat of beer and a platter of fried food, which of the 92 Grey Cups staged over time were the best.

Saskatchewan's 43-40 win over Hamilton in the 1989 game is considered by many to the classic, although some insist Toronto's 43-37 victory over Edmonton in 1996, B.C.'s patriotic 26-23 decision over an all-American Baltimore side in 1994 or Edmonton's 38-36 win over Toronto in 1987 were more riveting.

Old timers will argue the 1958 contest, a 35-28 Bomber victory over Hamilton, was the most entertaining. Or that the Fog Bowl, played over two days in 1962 before Winnipeg edged the Ticats 28-27, was just as fascinating.

There have also been superb Grey Cup festivals—like the two games in Regina in 1995 and 2003, the three staged in Edmonton in 1984, 1997 and 2002—that are the keys to great championship weeks.

So where do the two Grey Cups held in Winnipeg, back in 1991 and then in 1998, rank among the 92? Truthfully, they are right up there among the best.

But they also came along at critical times in the CFL's history, proving again that the lifeblood of the grand ol' loop lies here on the Prairies.

The '91 championship, the first where a CFL team and city actually bid for the rights—the price tag was $3 million—was brought to Winnipeg amidst great criticism from outside the Manitoba capital.

How can the league's marquee event, many vehemently protested, be held in a town that freezes over in October and doesn't begin to thaw until April?

That argument was only further fuelled by an ice storm that hammered Winnipeg three weeks before the game, forcing the Blue Bombers and Eskimos to play on a 90-yard field because the playing surface couldn't be completely cleared before kickoff.

Fact is, the '91 game was a life saver for the CFL —especially after the disaster of the 1990 game in Vancouver in which the announced crowd was 46,968 but with the actual attendance closer to 35,000 in cavernous B.C. Place.

The league and its showcase event needed a breath of fresh, crisp air. And the '91 game came along at the right time, pumping life back into the party and serving up the template for the successful championships that followed.

"One thing this year's Grey Cup has made clear in my mind," said then-Toronto Argonaut GM Mike McCarthy, "is the Grey Cup isn't glitz and glamour, it's old-fashioned hoopla. The Grey Cup isn't about the $150 a plate royal dinner, it's about last night's foot stompin', tobacco-chewin', beer drinkin' blowout. The Grey Cup isn't about big, expensive parties. It's about Canadians having a rousing good time. That's what this Winnipeg Grey Cup is showing us. The people of Winnipeg have done a wonderful job."

McCarthy's Argonauts captured the 79th championship that frigid (-16C at kickoff) afternoon in front of 51,985 stuffed into an expanded Winnipeg Stadium. The presence of Rocket Ismail, the Argos' high-priced superstar, guaranteed that ESPN and CNN were in Winnipeg to document the game as were Toronto part-owners John Candy and Wayne Gretzky and Canadian actors Martin Short and Alan Thicke.

Now, convincing fans that the 1998 Grey Cup in Winnipeg was also vital to the CFL's survival is a much tougher sell, especially considering the attendance of 34,157 was the smallest since 1975.

But, also consider where the CFL was in 1997 before labelling the '98 championship a failure and chastising the Bombers efforts at repeating the hype that surrounded '91 game. At the 1996 Grey Cup in Hamilton there was open talk that it could be the CFL's last, what with franchises dying and the American expansion experiment dead. The 1997 game, in Edmonton, helped beat off the wolves at the CFL's door, but when no one stepped up to stage the '98 Grey Cup—there was considerable risk in fronting the $3.7 million guarantee the league wanted—the Bombers graciously agreed to play host and with less than 13 months lead-up time to prepare for the event.

Marketing the game was difficult, what with the '98 Brier already held in Winnipeg that spring and with ticket prices set much too high ($124.50 for the end zone, $183 for a grandstand seat) and with the upcoming 1999 World Junior Hockey Championships and 1999 Pan Am Games already circled on everyone's calendar.

What was worse for the Bombers is the team didn't just stumble out of the gate that season, but fell flat on their collective mugs with an 0-10 start, killing hometown Grey Cup sales.

"The fact this game isn't sold out isn't Winnipeg's fault," apologized Jeff Giles, then the CFL's chief operating officer. "We very much appreciate what Winnipeg has done. Winnipeg was the only city to make a formal application for this game. There was really no other place to go."

The game itself was a classic and amazingly began with a temperature of plus 10°C. Calgary kicker Mark McLoughlin, who grew up in Winnipeg, hit a 35-yard field goal with no time remaining for a 26-24 victory over Hamilton.

And now, with the 2006 game coming back to Winnipeg, organizers here are hoping the festival will be a mix of the best of '91 and '98, with a packed house watching a spectacular game in decent weather after a memorable week-long party.

"I believe it will be much different this time than in '98," said CFL commissioner Tom Wright in awarding the '06 game to Winnipeg. "The league has changed. The Bombers have changed. Nobody wanted the game then and so Winnipeg stepped up and said, 'OK, I will.' That was six to eight months before it happened. This is 25 months."

Ed Tait is a football writer with the Winnipeg Free Press.

MATT DUNIGAN: THAT INCREDIBLE GAME

BY ED TAIT

Sometimes the planets and stars align correctly, a player gets in a groove and well, magic just happens.

■ Strong-armed quarterback Matt Dunigan: *An amazing 713 yards passing in one game.*

The Winnipeg Blue Bombers have seen dozens of their players rise up and do the unthinkable, from Bob McNamara, Eddie James and Lorne Benson all scoring six touchdowns in a single game to Albert Johnson III racking up an astonishing 474 combined yards in one evening.

We now take you back to July 14, 1994, when Bomber quarterback Matt Dunigan delivered a performance that, to this day, still baffles those who were first-hand witnesses and causes nightmares to the members of the Edmonton Eskimo air defence.

The wind was light and the temperature a perfect 21°C when the Bombers and Eskimos met at Winnipeg Stadium for just their second game of the season and a rematch of the 1993 Grey Cup game—a tilt the CFL, in a confounding decision, did not have on its television schedule.

Officially, the 21,686 who filed through the turnstiles were there to honour Bomber all-star tackle and hometown boy Chris Walby, who was suiting up for his 200th CFL game. But by the end of the night Dunigan had left everyone's jaw on the ground by scorching the Eskimos for 713 yards through the air.

That's not a misprint: 7-1-3 passing yards, a pro football record which still stands.

"Those are gaudy numbers," said a dumbfounded Mike Kelly, then the Bomber offensive co-ordinator, afterward. "You never think in those terms, 700 is almost beyond the realm of comprehension. I've never seen anything like it."

Nobody had. Amazingly, less than a year earlier B.C. quarterback Danny Barrett had thrown for 601 yards in a game against Toronto—an effort which broke Sam Etcheverry's mark of 586 and had stood for 39 years.

The Bombers were 0-1 after losing in B.C. in their season opener and were facing the very real possibility of dropping to 0-2 with the defending Grey Cup champs in town. The Eskimos opened the scoring with a 25-yard Sean Fleming field goal, but that's when Dunigan & Co. went to work. By the time the evening was over the Bombers had not only won 50-35, they had racked up 792 yards net offence, the third-highest total in CFL history, while two Bomber pass catchers—Alfred Jackson

and David Williams—would smash James Murphy's club record of 229 yards receiving.

"These things just kind of happen," said Dunigan. "It's stupid to even think of numbers like this. In the huddle, Walby's yelling at me, 'you're on fire.' (The Eskimos) were trying to make us work it down the field a little more. Hey, the receivers made the plays, the offensive line gave me the opportunity to throw the ball."

Jackson finished with seven catches for 308 yards and four TDs (of 55, 54, 34 and 88 yards) while Williams pulled in 10 passes for 242 yards and one score. The Eskimos opened the game with a ton of man-to-man coverage, then switched to zone in the second half to try and prevent the aerial assault. It didn't matter.

"When he's hot, he's dynamite," said then-Eskimo head coach Ron Lancaster of Dunigan. "When a guy gets on a roll like that, he's hard to beat. He's just a great football player."

So, too, was Jackson, who first arrived in Winnipeg as a cornerback but was converted to offence by Cal Murphy. Jackson became so confident he could do damage that night, he went to Dunigan early in the game and insisted he could eat Eskimo defensive back Charles Wright alive.

"I knew from the second series that if Matt could get me the ball something was there," said Jackson. "I told him if you lay it out there I'll run under it. It was unbelievable. I never thought 300 yards was possible."

And Murphy, who had seen just about everything during decades in the game, didn't think 713 yards passing was possible either. "I can't remember it ever happening," Murphy said. "That was a phenomenal night by both of them. At one point Matt said something about running the ball and I said, 'Are you kidding?'"

Ed Tait is a football writer for the Winnipeg Free Press.

■ Matt Dunigan: *Stretches for touchdown against Edmonton.*

need all the individual talent in the world. You need guys who want to do it for each other."

But the Grey Cup hangover would not last long for the Bombers. Riley, a two-time Coach of the Year in four years wearing the headset, left the club in January for a gig with the San Antonio Riders of the World League of American Football, as well as subsequent fame and fortune in the NFL. After an exhaustive search Murphy finally turned to an old friend to lead the Bombers in defence of their championship by naming former Detroit Lions boss Darryl Rogers as head coach for the '91 campaign.

That Bomber side, however, will hardly be remembered as gracious champions. There was in-fighting almost from the first moment training camp opened and by the time the leaves turned that fall, the club was a house divided because of the players' ongoing frustration with a tight-wad general manager and a lame-duck coach.

What was worse, the Grey Cup game would be played here in Winnipeg for the first time ever that November. And the rabid Bomber faithful desperately wanted the home side be in that contest.

KEEP YOUR EYES ON THE BALL: A WOMAN IN THE LOCKER ROOM

BY JUDY OWEN

When sports reporters are asked what it's like to watch games for a living, most people want to know what the athletes are like—who's nice, who's a jerk?

When a female sports reporter is asked the same question, there's usually an unspoken question they really want answered: What's it like to go into a locker room? When it comes to reporting on the Blue Bombers, the answer is wide-ranging.

One day I was covering a Bomber road trip when some info came my way about former head coach Jeff Reinebold's tenuous hold on his job.

I needed a couple quotes from him after the game, but by the time I tracked him down he was heading into the shower room off the coaches' change room.

Deadline looming, I walked past the other coaches to the shower room doorway and started asking him questions as he stood in front of the mirror. I'll add here that he had on a towel.

Interview done, I turned around and exited the room past the slightly surprised, but grinning, coaches.

Say what you will about Reinebold's coaching ability, but when it came to dealing with the media he got high marks for accessibility. It was a bonus that he was usually a good quote, too.

Had the tip come down during, say, the Cal Murphy reign, chances are I wouldn't even have made it into the coaches' room.

■ **Bomber celebration after 1984 Grey Cup:** ***Enter locker room at your own risk.***

Winnipeg Football Club

When I began covering the Bombers regularly in the mid-1990s, the locker room was closed to all media, male or female.

Murphy had put up the roadblock because of a complaint from a female radio reporter about her access to the team.

Rather than deal with that, he just shut the door. Some players were brought out for interviews, but that limited your selection and you lost the atmosphere of the room.

Eventually the room was re-opened to both sexes, albeit reluctantly. Murphy would often walk through to, I think, check on how the female reporters were acting and how the players were handling it.

Frankly, I've never had problems with players not wanting my presence in the locker room. Today, most will throw on a towel when they see me coming. In the cramped visiting team's dressing room, often I'll hear a player yell, "Lady in the room," and players will reach for a towel.

Most, I hope, appreciate that I'm conscious of their privacy. I try to keep my eyes on the floor when I'm walking around between interviews, and turn my back to the room while waiting to talk to a player. I like to say that I'm in there to get a quote, not a thrill.

One of the occasions when my gender is acknowledged is when a coach or player swears. They'll quickly turn to me and apologize. Not necessary. I've heard just about everything.

Having a thick skin is a must. There are some players who think reporters are the enemy, no matter their gender. After all, most of us have never reached the level they have—especially a female—so how could we possibly know anything about the game?

Case in point was when I did my annual *Winnipeg Sun* mid-season report card for the team during Reinebold's first year. Most units got F's or D's, not surprising when you consider their dismal 1-8 record.

When I went into the locker room a few days later to talk to one linebacker about something unrelated, he started yelling at me, calling me a "back-stabbing leech" for the D grade I'd given the linebackers. I walked away. No use wasting my time arguing. He was eventually traded. I shed no tears.

After all, I'm not about to throw in the towel. Unless, of course, it's for someone to use as a wrap.

Judy Owen is a former reporter with the Winnipeg Sun.

But the ticking time bomb in the Bomber locker room exploded in the fall when linebacker Tyrone Jones staged a one-man protest by skipping out of practice because, among other things, he and his teammates were weary of "having to wear Mack Herron's old jock" and running over to Eaton's to buy socks on game day. One of the other main beefs, pardon the awful pun, was apparently the cheap pre-game meals Jones complained had "no meat in the spaghetti sauce."

But the troubles were much more deep-rooted than that and while the players set up a committee to deal with the complaints, nothing was ever resolved and it was with those distractions the team carried into November in an attempt to defend their Grey Cup title.

In front of a frigid but capacity crowd of 51,985 at Winnipeg Stadium and sporting a shoulder that had turned to mush because of repeated poundings, Dunigan had his wing frozen with pain killers and still managed to throw for two scores while rushing seven times for 44 yards.

After finishing 9-9, the Bombers easily dispatched Ottawa 26-8 in the East semi-final, setting up a showdown with the Argos in Toronto. The game was so anticipated that 50,380 packed the SkyDome, but they were hardly treated to a CFL classic. The Bombers would spit up the ball nine times in their 42-3 mauling as Burgess was yanked after completing just 3 of 14 for 39 yards while being picked off twice.

As fate would have it, his counterpart across the field, Dunigan, was brilliant that day and a week later in leading the Argos to the championship over Calgary in one of the grittiest performances in Grey Cup history.

In front of a frigid but capacity crowd of 51,985 at Winnipeg Stadium and sporting a shoulder that had turned to mush because of repeated poundings, Dunigan had his wing frozen with pain killers and still managed to throw for two scores while rushing seven times for 44 yards. Several of Dunigan's teammates were in tears before the game while watching their leader squirm in agony on the training table as he took the needles that would help alleviate some of the pain.

Ken Gigliotti, Winnipeg Free Press

■ **Rick House:** ***A receiver who rarely took his eyes off the ball.***

"I just didn't know if I was going to get that close again," Dunigan would explain later. "I thought, if I can play and it's not going to take away from the team's chances of winning and I can contribute and be a factor then I'll do whatever it takes. Let's fire it up and go."

Interestingly, that Cup performance, and the way Dunigan gutted and filleted the Bombers in the East Final, spawned an idea that began percolating in Murphy's head that winter and leads us to our next stop...

■ Cal Murphy: *From head coach to general manager and back again.*

OF HEART TRANSPLANTS, AMERICAN EXPANSION AND BIG NUMBERS

Cal Murphy, along with the help of the Bomber landlords Winnipeg Enterprises Corporation, pulled off a major coup heading into the '92 season by signing the free agent Matt Dunigan to a $500,000 a season contract.

It was a brilliant move, adding one of the CFL's elite pivots to a club many thought still was of championship calibre despite the soap opera that was the '91 season. Not so brilliant was letting the much-cheaper backup QB Danny McManus sign with B.C. at the end of the season.

Dunigan was the perfect fit for the Bombers, breathing life into a stagnant offence, generating a buzz about the team off the field and playing an instrumental role in helping smooth over the rough edges of what had become a team divided. He was superb from his very first game in Blue and Gold, leading the Bombers to a dramatic 36-33 OT win in Hamilton in Week 1.

Sadly, the man who played such a vital role in bringing him to Winnipeg could only follow the action from his bed at University Hospital in London, Ontario. Murphy, who had decided to replace Rogers with himself as head coach for the '92 season, was admittedly a little worn out during training camp that June. But a suspected angina attack in early July turned out to be much worse than initially feared and before long the native Winnipegger was on an operating table desperately needing a new heart—but with no donor in sight.

His life, frankly, was hanging in the balance as his heart had deteriorated so quickly he was undergoing emergency bypass surgery that would have kept him alive for only hours when the organ from the victim of a motorcycle accident became available, literally with no time to spare. "It's absolutely amazing, it really is," said Murphy months later. "I know this might sound corny, but sometimes I look at the obituaries in the paper and I say to myself, 'Why not me?' The Grim Reaper should have had me."

But Murphy's absence during the '92 season obviously left the Bombers rudderless and in another potentially explosive situation. Murphy asked long-time assistant Urban Bowman to take over the head coaching duties while Lyle Bauer, just a few months from his retirement from the offensive line and his appointment as assistant GM, moved into the big chair. That pair would amazingly keep the Bombers from imploding, although the club would be up and down like a toilet seat at a house party all season.

■ Cal Murphy watches practice: *While visiting from Regina where he scouts for the Indianapolis Colts.*

■ Ouch: *At training camp sometimes scrimmages can be as rough as a real game.*

MILT STEGALL: THE PROFESSIONAL

BY ED TAIT

He'll be a first-ballot inductee into the Canadian Football Hall of Fame and will be remembered as one of the greatest receivers ever to play the three-down game.

And, yes, Milt Stegall has the obvious natural gifts that separate the greats from the average pros —the soft hands of a safe cracker, the superb sense of timing and a fiery competitive desire.

But to truly understand what makes Stegall outstanding, you need watch just 10 minutes or so of any Bomber practice on any day during the season.

The man, simply put, does not take one solitary play off whether the sun is scorching or the wind is howling. Every single repetition is done at full speed, from start to finish. And it's that dedication to his craft that leaves even the greenest of rookies wide-eyed in wonderment—who is this guy and why is he always busting his hump?

"Why? I do it because I want to give myself every opportunity," explained Stegall one day last summer. "I don't want any excuses as to why I didn't do well. Every time I step on the field I want to be prepared mentally, physically. You never know what that guy across from you has done to make himself better."

Stegall's monk-like approach to sport—he doesn't eat red meat or sweets and works out roughly 360 days a year (including his honeymoon a couple years back)—comes from his folks.

His late father Garland was an engineer who dabbled in real estate and owned a grocery store while his mother Betty was a nurse. Together they did absolutely everything they could to make their family's lives better and to help put Milt through college.

"My drive comes from my parents, seeing the things they did, how they worked and provided and for me and my brothers and sisters," said Stegall, the Bombers all-time leading receiver. "They gave us a great home and great schooling. They worked hard. They sacrificed."

How dominant has Stegall been since first arriving in Winnipeg in 1995?

Consider that in the 2004 season the veteran slotback pulled in 68 catches for 1,121 yards and six touchdowns in 16 games—and it was thought he was in a major-league slump. But, remember, during Stegall's remarkable career he has a startling 111 touchdowns in just 139 games, a spectacular ratio for a receiver.

And Stegall was never more spectacular than in 2002 when he hauled in 105 passes for 1,862 yards and a CFL single season record 23 touchdowns. That year he became the sixth Bomber to win the Most Outstanding Player Award after Don Jonas (1971), Dieter Brock (1980,1981), Willard Reaves (1984), James Murphy (1986), Tom Clements (1987) and Khari Jones (2001).

All that said, all the gaudy numbers and his place among CFL legends is not what drives Stegall. Never has. No, Stegall is after the elusive championship ring—something he has never won as a pro or in college.

"I'd trade it all in for just one Grey Cup," Stegall said. "If you said I could have one Grey Cup ring for all these records, I'd trade it in a second. I haven't been on a championship team my whole life. That's the only reason I'm playing.

■ Milt Stegall: *Simply gets first downs and touchdowns whenever he's on the field.*

Winnipeg Free Press

"This personal stuff is what you look at down the road, after the season or when you retire. It means nothing. You ask a guy like Dan Marino and I guarantee you he'd turn in all the records he broke for just one Super Bowl ring. You don't play for the records, you play this game to win games and win championships."

Ed Tait is a football writer for the Winnipeg Free Press.

With Dunigan battling injuries, the club would start three different QBs that season—including Garza and Danny McManus—but after falling to 6-7 in early October, reeled off five straight regular-season wins and then spanked Hamilton 59-11 in the East Final.

Unfortunately, that's when all the good karma ended. The Bombers were no match for the Calgary Stampeders in the Grey Cup and the marquee QB duel featuring Dunigan and Doug Flutie was a bust. Flutie was superb, throwing for 480 yards and two scores while Dunigan was only six-of-19 for 47 yards before being replaced by McManus. The Stamps led 17-zip at halftime en route to an easy 24-10 win, the first of the Bombers three consecutive championship game losses.

With corporate revenue dying and several teams on life support, then-commissioner Larry Smith made the desperate decision to expand to the United States.

That winter would see the CFL undergo a dramatic and controversial change, and not without the vehement protests of Murphy, who had returned home in November, and the Bomber organization. With corporate revenue dying and several teams on life support, then-commissioner Larry Smith made the desperate decision to expand to the United States. Only the Bombers were against the move.

The whole affair was a cash grab, some still say necessary for survival, but it was poorly planned and, save for Baltimore, the markets could have cared less about three-down football. In the end, the experiment was one embarrassing fiasco after another, beginning with Smith announcing at the 1993 Coach of the Year banquet that the San Antonio had suddenly backed out for the upcoming season—leaving just the Sacramento Gold Miners as the lone expansion entry— before he ducked away on a freight elevator to avoid the press and left Fred Anderson, the classy Miners' owner, to answer questions and defend the CFL's honour all at the same time.

Over the next three seasons the Bombers would play games in Sacramento, Baltimore, Shreveport,

Birmingham and Las Vegas while the league bopped all over the U.S. map, also setting up in Memphis and San Antonio while promising franchises to Orlando and Jackson, Miss. but burying them before they even took a breath because the financial backing was not in place. Only the Baltimore Stallions, headed by Don Matthews, seemed to put down roots and instantly became a rival for the Bombers, who would play in Maryland four times—including one preseason game and in the '95 playoffs—all to healthy crowds.

Along the way there were some hilarious moments and some unimaginable lows for the league, most of which severely damaged the grand ol' loop's already-tarnished credibility.

There was indifference from folks in the U.S. and ignorance to the glory of the Canadian game and of their northern neighbour in general –

There was Walby doing an impromptu stand-up routine while answering questions at a pre-game press conference in Sacramento, leaving media who had never heard of this large man from Winnipeg's North End, rolling in the aisles in laughter.

There was the cheesy Vegas lounge singer who, before a Saskatchewan-Las Vegas Posse game in Sin City, belted out 'O Canada!' to the tune of 'O Christmas Tree.'

There were the tiny end zones in Memphis, the Shreveport Pirates housing their players in training camp above a barn for circus animals and the awful fan support in Vegas—the Bombers lone game there drew just 2,350 with an estimated 1,800 of that total Manitobans who had flocked down on charters—before the Posse were forced to play their final regular-season home game in Edmonton after the league took control of the franchise when the bills weren't being paid.

Above all, there was indifference from folks in the U.S. and ignorance to the glory of the Canadian game and of their northern neighbour in general—perhaps best exemplified by a restaurant waitress in Shreveport who, when told by a handful of reporters they were from Winnipeg during one visit in '94, replied: 'I just studied Canada in gee-ography. Betcha I can name all 10 providences (sic).

THE LONG AND WINDING ROAD

BY BOB CAMERON

I owe my career to drugs. But before parents' jaws drop, read on.

After winning the Hec Crighton Trophy as a quarterback/punter at Acadia University and being the first round draft choice of the Edmonton Eskimos, I thought that I would be a shoo-in to make it in the CFL. Boy was I wrong. The long and winding road began in 1977 at the Eskimos training camp. The team was going into the year having lost punter Garry Lefebvre to retirement. No problem. The job was mine. Little did I know that a grade 11 student—a freak of nature with size 16 feet—would be joining me in camp. You may have heard of him, his name was Hank Ilesic. I couldn't believe it, he was 17-years-old and he could out-punt me by ten yards a kick. But as it happened neither Hank nor I began the season as Edmonton's punter, CFL veteran Gerald Kunyk won the job. But he only played five games and then Hank, or 'Bigfoot' as he was called, was brought back.

After getting cut by Edmonton I drove south to Calgary where I tried out with the Stampeders. The league had 32 man rosters back then and the Stamps were looking for a guy who could play another position as well as punt. And even though I was a better punter than the other guy, Bill Palmer, he could also play linebacker and I was gone. Oh

■ **Blue Bomber long-time punter Bob Cameron:** ***The best 'into-the-wind' punter in CFL history.***

yeah, Bill could do more than just play football, he could also father NFL quarterbacks—he's Jesse's (New York Giants) dad.

Then in January of 1978 I played in the first Can-Am Bowl in Florida where I was approached by a Philadelphia Eagles scout. He invited me to their spring camp and I was cut again. Although bruised, I was still hopeful of playing pro that year because I was signed by the Ottawa Rough Riders to compete with my old friend Gerald Kunyk. After playing four solid exhibition games and out-kicking Gerald every day in practice I knew I had the team made. Even the *Ottawa Citizen* had me penciled in as the punter. Unbelievably, the head coach, George Brancato, said that they would be going with Gerald because 'he would be more consistent.' I was devastated. Then another tryout that same year, this time with Hamilton, failed when their incumbent, Nick Jambrosic, had the game of his life with me breathing down his neck. You guessed it, I was cut again. I decided to head back to Acadia University for my final year of college football.

After playing in the 1979 Can-Am Bowl and winning the game MVP award as a punter, I was signed by the Buffalo Bills. It was now the summer of 1979 and Buffalo had invited nine punters to camp. By the middle of camp there were only two punters standing, Rusty Jackson and me. It all came down to the final exhibition game against the Pittsburgh Steelers. I punted in the first half and Jackson the second. Oh well, at least I got to play on the same field as Terry Bradshaw. Back to Canada.

So there I was, three years of trying out, seven teams, and no work. But then in December of 1979, while driving through a snow storm to Calgary, I heard a voice on the radio. The reporter said that Bernie Ruoff, the all-star punter/placekicker for the Winnipeg Blue Bombers had just been arrested on a marijuana charge and had been traded to Hamilton. At that moment, I thought that I just might get one more chance. I didn't know it then, but another young kicker, 150 miles to the north of me in Edmonton, had also heard the same report.

I was invited to the Blue Bombers training camp in the spring of 1980. I was one of only two punters in camp and the team was hoping that Walt Passaglia, Lui's brother, could fill in as placekicker. But after following what was happening in other the CFL training camps, I soon realized that my time in Winnipeg would be short-lived. The Toronto Argonauts had two outstanding veteran dual kickers in camp and the Bombers were looking to quickly snap up the guy that the Argo's released. With the way things had gone for me up to that point, I figured my days were again numbered. Then a stocky little kicker walked into the locker room.

It was the day after our first exhibition game, and Trevor Kennerd had just been cut by the Saskatchewan Roughriders. His first kicking session on the grass at Winnipeg Stadium was all I needed to renew my hope of making the team. Man he could kick the ball. It was at an exhibition game in Toronto, where we were playing against those same two Argo kickers, that Trevor nailed both our jobs with a monster 57 yard field goal on the last play of the half. He went 8 for 9 over the next two games and after three years and seven tryouts I was finally a professional punter.

Life was good...for about five games. Then someone that I knew all too well breezed into Winnipeg—Gerald Kunyk. The Bombers were struggling and Ray Jauch thought a shake-up was in order so he released me and handed the job to Gerald. This cut was the deepest as it had occurred prior to my first game ever in my hometown of Hamilton. In fact, I was cut right after the pre-game meal, four hours before game time. All my family and friends were going to be at the game to cheer me on and it had happened again. That was the eighth time I had been cut. Eight times! Needless to say, I was totally frustrated that day and didn't even go to the game.

After the game, Trev and I roamed the empty streets of Hamilton until the early morning and he said something that kindled some hope. Gerald had played a poor game and Trevor felt the competition for the punting job would be back on.

The next week, after gruelling daily punting sessions, I finally earned the job. I knew that if I could just hang on for one year that I could play for ten. Well, twenty-three years and three Grey Cup championships later I retired. What a ride it was. My new life as a husband, father, and real estate investor in Winnipeg is great. And don't worry, Gerald Kunyk isn't in the real estate business, he's a teacher.

Bob Cameron recently retired as the Bomber punter after a 73, we mean 23 year career.

Winnipeg Free Press

There's Sas-kat-CHEE-wan, Kweee-bec, the one that starts with Prince and those two up north that nobody goes to.'

All those sideshows aside, the '93 and '94 campaigns were two of the most electrifying in Bomber history. The team would go 27-9 over that span (14-4 in '93, 13-5 a year later) and, in the process, re-wrote much of the club's offensive record book. But, alas, there was another November nightmare as Dunigan ripped up his Achilles tendon in '93 and a year later they would be the victims of horrible luck in a divisional final loss to Baltimore.

Needing to play mistake-free football in the Grey Cup a week later against the Eskimos, the Bombers were atrocious early, handling the football like it was a wet bar of soap while falling behind 21-0.

In '93 the Bombers were cruising along at 11-4 after having locked up first in the East for weeks—Hamilton would finish second that year at a laughable 6-12—when they faced Sacramento in mid October with nothing at stake but keeping the rust at bay before the playoffs. Midway through the third quarter Dunigan hit David Williams for a TD, establishing a new team record with his 36th aerial strike of the season, but on the next possession he went down like he had been shot by a sniper. And the prognosis couldn't have been worse: a severed Achilles tendon that ended his season.

Sammy Garza, who had picked up the nickname 'Sammy Son-in-Law' after marrying one of Murphy's daughters, gave the Bombers decent quarterbacking in wins over Ottawa and Toronto to end the regular season but the offence had lost its explosiveness with Dunigan on the shelf.

That was never more evidenced than in the East Final when the Bombers barely edged the Ticats, a team they had beaten three times that season by a combined score of 136-32, by just 20-19.

Needing to play mistake-free football in the Grey Cup a week later against the Eskimos, the Bombers were atrocious early, handling the football like it was a wet bar of soap while falling behind 21-0. They would rally in the second half, closing to within a touchdown with 2 1/2 minutes remaining, but couldn't close the deal and fell 33-23.

It was the second devastating finish to a campaign in as many seasons, but the heartache would only sting even more a year later.

■ **Khari Jones:** ***Celebrating one of the many touchdowns scored while he was Winnipeg's starting quarterback.***

LIVING A DREAM

BY TREVOR KENNERD

■ All-star placekicker Trevor Kennerd: *Won three Grey Cup championships and kicked the winning field goal in the 1988 Grey Cup game.*

Winnipeg Free Press

"Hey Forrest, I'm open!" Only 11 years old, but I had just beaten Edmonton Eskimo defensive back Dick Dupuis with a slick post-corner move. I wore a plain white t-shirt with the number '25' scrawled on the back. I was Terry Evanshen of the Calgary Stampeders. My twin brother Forrest (Peter Liske), threw a perfect spiral that I hauled in just before stepping out onto the front sidewalk. "Touchdown!" The roar of 25,000 fans on 86th Avenue echoed in my head as I jogged back to the front steps.

This was the joy of growing up in the suburbs of east Edmonton; of being 11-years-old and dreaming of playing in the CFL. The days of going to Eskimo games, sitting in the 'Woodward's Knothole Gang' and watching stars such as Lancaster, Reed, Kapp, Young, Ploen, Raimey, Nielsen, Minnick, Luzzi, Harris, Thomas, and Kerbow. The dream has been shared by millions of Canadian kids. OK, millions more are dreaming about scoring the winning goal in the Stanley Cup, but those are the kids that can skate. For the rest of us, the CFL is Canada.

The CFL is a place where people from all over the continent–players and fans alike–come together to play, cheer and 'grab grass and growl.' They all share in the dream. Many American players have made their living here and found a special home to raise their families. For young Canadian football players, the CFL is something to shoot for. It is where your dreams can take you. And once there, you are allowed to be an 11-year-old kid playing the game you love–and even make some decent money to boot (pun intended).

It's hard to describe the emotions of pulling on a Winnipeg Blue Bombers jersey for the first time. It was 1980, in my birthplace of Calgary–the home of the team that consumed my boyhood fantasies. I was a Blue Bomber now and everything was in focus. The dream was a reality.

To make it to the Canadian Football League. To be a Blue Bomber. To have teammates like Cameron, Poplawski, Murphy, House, Bonk, Battle, Helton, Walby, Brock, Clements and so many others. To share in the sheer ecstasy of three Grey Cup championships. To be welcomed as a citizen of Winnipeg, Manitoba. To raise three strong boys who also love the game. This is a wonderful dream and it's what the Canadian Football League is all about.

"Hey dad, I'm open!"

The '94 Bombers were one of the best outfits ever assembled in team history. Featuring stars like Dunigan, Blaise Bryant, Gerald Wilcox, Greg Clark, Miles Gorrell, Walby and others. Not only did that squad finish 13-5, it set a club record with 651 points scored, despite Dunigan being on the shelf, again, for seven games. By comparison that's 203 points more than the 2004 team.

Winnipeg finished just two points ahead of Baltimore in the East standings, setting up a classic showdown in the '94 division final. The teams struggled offensively despite two rosters jammed with offensive talent and the Bombers would fall 14-12 after two key developments both went against the home side. The Bombers would recover an apparent Mike Pringle fumble at their goal line, only to have the play missed by the officials. Then, with the team driving for a potential game-winning score, horrified fans watched a Dunigan pass clang off the crossbar with a wide-open Wilcox waiting in the end zone.

Those kind of scenes, unfortunately, would repeat themselves less than 10 years later when three more solid Bomber teams of 2001, 2002 and 2003, would get close but never get their names engraved on the Cup.

But, before we fast-forward to more shots at glory, we must first revisit the decline of a once-powerful outfit....

■ **CFL all-star offensive tackle Chris Walby:** ***Has taken his football knowledge and quick wit to the broadcast booth.***

OH, THE HORROR...A TEAM'S FALL FROM THE ELITE

Many Americans playing football in Canada often felt like strangers in a strange land. And, we suppose, Dunigan—even though he had played in the CFL since 1983—felt no different in 1995, especially with the new U.S. owners flashing all those Ben Franklins in front of him.

So it was no surprise when Dunigan left the Bombers in the spring of '95 to join up with the expansion Birmingham Barracudas, owned by insurance magnate Art Williams and playing out of legendary Legion Field, home of the Alabama Crimson Tide. Dunigan bolted for a huge contract worth an estimated $750,000.

Without Dunigan the Bombers were cooked. Garza entered the '95 campaign as the starter but was sent to Ottawa before Labour Day. And, as was the case with the team in the late '80s, the search for a new pivot began. Reggie Slack, Shawn Moore and Kevin McDougal would all start games for the team after Garza's departure, but this was a b-a-a-a-d football side that surrendered a club-record 653 points that season, including a shocking 65-17 loss in front of just 11,000 in Shreveport.

Winnipeg would finish fifth in the North Division at 7-11, before crossing over and being spanked 36-21 by the eventual Grey Cup champion Baltimore Stallions in the South Division Semifinals.

Winnipeg Free Press

■ **Milt Stegall reaches for one vs the Argonauts:** ***Big play machine with a knack for beating double coverage.***

The Bombers desperately tried to put a band-aid on their QB woes by dealing with Toronto to land veteran Kent Austin prior to the '96 season. But Austin, then 33, was in obvious decline and a shadow of the QB who had thrown for 6,225 yards with Saskatchewan in '92. Winnipeg would finish 9-9 that year and then rolled into Edmonton to face the 11-7 Eskimos in the division semifinal.

The contest was played on a field covered in snow and ice but the Bombers' poor footwear was simply a game-day sidebar that temporarily masked the team's many problems. The Bombers were down 31-1 at halftime en route to a 68-7 loss, the worst in franchise history and the most points ever surrendered by a CFL team in the playoffs.

There were two scenes from the debacle that were particularly appalling to Bomber fans: the shot of the club's executive delivering new cleats to the sidelines with the blowout already started after scrambling to a sporting goods store, and of how quickly many of the players threw up the white flag in surrender.

Afterward, offensive lineman Brett MacNeil stood in the middle of the Bomber dressing room and unleashed a now infamous post-massacre rant that was delivered loudly enough for everyone within a city block to hear. As it turned out, MacNeil's thinking would only foreshadow the team's free-fall over the next three years.

"What happened? We got our asses kicked," said MacNeil "A lot of guys are battling out there but we've got a lot of pussies on our team, too. It showed...When you've got half your team cowering by the heaters in a game as big as this you've got to question some of the character of the guys on this team...You need tough guys on a football team. It's a sport that's not for the weak of heart...We better come back stronger next season or we're going to be in the basement. This hurts. It's embarrassing."

Oh, but the hurt and the embarrassment was only beginning...Within five days of the slaughter, the Bomber executive opted to make a dramatic change, sweeping Murphy out of the GM and head coaching positions after 14 years as the face of the franchise.

"It's going to be very weird around here now," said Walby. "It's like Christmas without the Christmas tree. You always expect him to be there." And the new face taking Murphy's place? Well, grab your arm rests folks because here's where the ride gets very, very choppy...

THE REIGN OF ERROR...

Jeff Reinebold had never been a head coach before he arrived in Winnipeg. Ever. Not in college and not as a pro. And, during his 32 games as the Bomber boss over the next two years before he was canned, it showed almost weekly.

But while his resumé may have been thin, he had the gift of the gab and the kind of personality that made people instantly gravitate to him like a pied piper or, some would say later, a cult leader. He was charming and well spoken, sported a permanent tan, with tattoos and ear-rings rounding out his ensemble. In short, he was the anti-Cal Murphy. And before the 1997 season had even started, he would own this town as the team's new head coach and director of football operations.

Perhaps adhering to the old saying it's better to burn out than to fade away, Reinebold quickly began work on what he brashly predicted would become a powerful contender. And while his motives to clean house weren't entirely wrong given what happened at the end of '96, his bravado would end up chomping him regularly on the backside over the next two years. "It ain't about making a football team here," said Reinebold six months before he would coach his first game with the Bombers. "This isn't about going 9-9. This is about kicking everybody's ass. Then it's about lining up and saying, 'Who's next?' I'm talking about creating a dynasty."

Instead, his legacy is the toxic mushroom cloud he left behind with the Bombers. In his defence, Reinebold was saddled with a football team that was in serious decline on the field and with some enormous concerns off it. As well, the CFL in 1997 was bleeding badly, its image in tatters after the U.S. expansion experiment exploded in their mugs and then, in 1996, the folding of the Ottawa Rough Riders.

It was in that environment that Reinebold was not only charged with rebuilding a team, but with trying to put some sizzle into another desperate Bomber season-ticket drive.

He tried. My, how he tried. But with a relatively inexperienced staff and still no bona fide quarterback—they would start McDougal and Chris Vargas in '97, and then the immortal trio of T.J. Rubley, Kevin Mason and Troy Kopp in '98 – it was a team destined to fail.

Of course, Reinebold hardly helped himself, either. He immediately hitched his wagon to the unproven McDougal, sent the team's Most Outstanding Player in '96—linebacker K.D. Williams—to Saskatchewan; announced the free-agent signing of receiver Alfred Jackson and then watched him re-sign with B.C. later that week when

■ **(From left) Head coach Jeff Reinebold and offensive coordinator Joe Paopao: *'We will dominate the CFL'.***

Winnipeg Free Press

SHORT YARDAGE

Did you know: Bomber's all-time leading scorer, Troy Westwood, is Manitoba's 'Walter Mitty'. He has tried tap dancing, boxing, writing poetry, race car driving, and First Nations music.

the deal wasn't officially agreed upon; flunked Miles Gorrell and Michael Richardson in their pre-camp physicals; traded slotback Gerald Wilcox for socks and a jockstrap to be named later and cut proven regulars like linebacker Greg Clark, fullback Dean Lytle and defensive end John Kropke during training camp.

To further confound matters, Walby and Stan Mikawos—two mainstays and clubhouse leaders—retired before the '97 season while Angelo Snipes was a hold out and Charlie Clemons bolted for the NFL.

"Hey, if we're completely screwed up and 18 weeks later we're looking at a 5-13 record with nothing headed in the right direction then I'll be man enough to say, 'Yeah, I was wrong.' But I don't see that right now." He would within a few weeks, however.

"I hope I don't disappoint you, but I don't spend a lot of time thinking about what if, what should've, could've, would've," said Reinebold in his farewell press conference. "I made the decisions. I live with those decisions. Hold me accountable."

The effects of the massive overhaul showed the moment the Bombers started playing real games and by the time the season ended they were a woeful 4-14. They would lose six games by a touchdown or less, but also dropped four games where the margin was better than 21 points.

And yet, fan support for the man and his vision continued to grow. So when the team ended the season with a 55-19 blowout win over Saskatchewan, there was guarded optimism for 1998, despite the fact the '97 side had become the first since 1979 to miss the playoffs.

Still, the same major problem persisted through that winter—even after the signing of Rubley, who came to Winnipeg after being named the Most Valuable Offensive Player in the World League: the quarterbacking was shaky and the depth of Canadian talent was suspect.

What was worse, with the CFL teetering on extinction (many who gathered for the '97 Grey Cup were whispering it could be the league's last) the Bomber organization opted to buy the rights to the '98 championship when no other team stepped up to the plate, but with very little lead up time to market and sell it.

Sadly, the team's chances of competing for the title in their own park were gone right after the coin flip in the first game. Winnipeg was 0-5 by the end of July and 0-10 after Labour Day. And although offensive co-ordinator Joe Paopao fell on a sword to temporarily protect his boss, Reinebold's firing was a fait accompli with crowds dwindling and the team falling deeper into the abyss. The end, mercifully, came in early October and with the team wallowing in the cellar at 2-12.

"I hope I don't disappoint you, but I don't spend a lot of time thinking about what if, what should've, could've, would've," said Reinebold in his farewell press conference. "I made the decisions. I live with those decisions. Hold me accountable."

Within hours of his dismissal, the Bombers began courting Eric Tillman as their next GM. That courtship would last well into November, but as Tillman mulled over the situation, the team also aggressively pursued another man, a man they had already left at the altar once before but who was still eager to get hitched...

FROM BAD BUSINESS TO GOOD BUSINESS

Dave Ritchie isn't a complicated man, nor is his approach to football: get your players to play better or, simply put, get better players. Stubbornly faithful, almost to a fault, his football philosophy

7

■ Charles Roberts running away from a Hamilton defender. "Blink" has proven that size really doesn't matter as he routinely rips up CFL defences.

Winnipeg Free Press

would best be described by the note he kept taped to the mini-fridge in his office during his 5 1/2 years as the Bomber head coach. It read: 'Loyalty above all else, except honour.'

Like Reinebold, Ritchie was considered a players' coach and regularly had his troops ready to knock over walls for him. But, the similarity between the two coaches essentially ended there. Where Reinebold was new age, as quick to quote Bob Marley as to draw up a defensive scheme, Ritchie was a Bible-thumpin', bent-nosed old schooler who came with a proven track record and a Grey Cup ring as the leader of the '94 B.C. Lions.

He brought with him a respected talent scout from the B.C. Lions, Brendan Taman, and together the two began rebuilding what was once one of the CFL's elite teams. But the depths of the problems were much worse than anybody could have imagined, with the talent wafer-thin and the business side in a shambles (with all the losing, season-ticket base had fallen to around 7,500 after reaching 17,700 in 1996). Just how bad was the picture? With projected losses estimated to creep near $900,000 that season—the ugly total was closer to $1.5 million by the time the final numbers were crunched—the team dumped Hall of Famer Ken Ploen from its sales force in September.

On the field, the first step was simply to make

What the organization needed in its new president was a face to lead the off-field charge; someone who would not-so-politely arm twist those who were beginning to doubt the franchise's value to the community.

the Bombers competitive again and the retooling began with the addition of some proven names like Cory Philpot, Barry Wilburn, Harold Nash, Jr., Robert Gordon, Tom Europe and quarterback Kerwin Bell, who was picked up in a trade from the Argos. No, Bell wasn't the fleetest of foot—his 40-yard dash was timed by a sun dial—but in '98 with the Argos he had the CFL's best quarterback-efficiency rating and a 67.2 completion percentage. Instantly, Bell beefed up the main trouble spot that had plagued the team since Dunigan's departure.

Winnipeg Free Press

■ **Bomber Head Coach Dave Ritchie:** ***Built a winning team in 2001 that just missed sipping from the Grey Cup that year.***

Still, the progress was painfully slow. The Bombers would drop their first game under the new regime 39-9 to Hamilton, but then thumped the Argos 47-27 in their next. As the summer wore on this squad would try to put up a brave fight all the while trying to save pennies at the same time. Sean Millington and Grant Carter were both jettisoned in salary-cap moves before Labour Day and while the team was still in the playoff hunt until the final week of the season and had doubled its win to total to six, there was no mistaking the concern: a 6-12 record that included eight losses of 20 points or more.

"I had a coach once, that when things weren't going well, he took us for a walk in the woods," said Ritchie, in one of his many classic mangled analogies. "We saw all the bugs and the bees and all that other crap, and then he sent us back to the barracks. We came out on the Saturday and played very well...Trouble is, with these guys we might take a walk in the woods and I might lose two or three of them. The people in the park might leave because they'd be worried the losing would rub off on them."

The ongoing on-field concerns would be overshadowed that winter, unfortunately, by another death-watch for the football team. This time, however, an aggressive approach was taken to changing the nasty cycle that kept repeating itself:

team loses money, goes hat in hand to the governments for help, then begs fans and corporate community for more support. The management structure was changed, with the volunteer president replaced by a full-time boss who would report to a board of directors. As well, a stakeholders agreement was established with the help of the provincial and civic governments, the CFL and Winnipeg Enterprises, with very specific goals aimed at attacking a massive debtload that had ballooned to $5.34 million.

Then the talent, the bravado and a cocksure attitude all came together for one marvelous stretch of football through to the late fall.

What the organization needed in its new president was a face to lead the off-field charge; someone who would not-so-politely arm twist those who were beginning to doubt the franchise's value to the community. And in Lyle Bauer they found the perfect candidate—a blue-jeans and boots guy, and a former centre and Bomber Hall of Famer who led the charge to attack the debt like he was back in football's trenches.

But Bauer understood the sales pitch would have a lot more oomph if the product on the field wasn't so awful. Charged with getting better in a hurry, Ritchie and Taman again attacked the offseason like rabid animals adding Juran Bolden, Brian Clark and Elfrid Payton in free agency, trading for Moe Elewonibi and Dave Mudge and unearthing starters like Albert Johnson III, Ron Warner, Brandon Dyson, Jamie Stoddard and Ryland Wickman. But it was Taman who pulled the trigger on a trade in February of 2000 that would hardly grab headlines across the nation at the time and yet would have a dramatic effect on the team's reversal of fortune.

■ Khari Jones drops back vs the Lions: *Set a club record with 46 touchdown passes in 2002.*

A STEAL OF A DEAL

Khari Jones was well down the depth chart with the Lions, almost an afterthought. But Taman liked the guy's intelligence, his perseverance and his skill set and so he shipped the team's best O-lineman, Christopher Perez, out west for Jones and a draft pick (which was later used to select Markus Howell).

Now, Bell was still the team's clear-cut starter as the '00 season began, but frustration mounted with four straight losses. Jones would make his first start in a 41-41 tie with the Argos and two weeks later was the team's clear-cut No. 1 gun. The results weren't instantaneous, but Jones brought a grip-it-and-rip-it approach to the quarterback position, playing each down like a guy working on his last chance to make a favourable impression.

"Let's be honest, the quarterback is more important than the GM, the head coach... everybody," said slotback Milt Stegall. "You don't have a quarterback, you can't win. Khari is not a rah-rah guy but his performance speaks for itself. You win games, the guys are going to like you whether you're a bumhead off the field or a nice guy."

At the same time, players like Bolden were bringing a brashness to the defensive side of the ball that was becoming contagious. The Bombers would go 5-3 in their final eight games to finish 7-10-1-1 and qualify for the playoffs for the first time since '96. Their first postseason contest came in Hamilton and, courtesy of a Troy Westwood field

Winnipeg Free Press

goal with two seconds left, the Bombers advanced to the division final in Montreal with their first playoff victory since 1994.

Winnipeg would jump to a 13-zip lead over the heavily-favoured Alouettes, who finished first at 12-6, but Jones was rattled by a late hit by Ed Philion and never really recovered. Neither did the Bombers, who fell 35-24.

But, for the first time in years, the club entered the offseason giddy about building on something. "This football team has been pretty good for the last 16 games (8-7-1, including the playoffs)," said Ritchie. "If we can start next season with the same drive, I think we'll be fine."

Little did he know just how much drive the '01 squad would have.... The 2001 Bomber season will be remembered as both one of the most exciting and frustrating in the team's existence.

Through the end of July their play was just average, as they went 2-2, but teased fans with their upside—especially Jones, who would later be named the league's Most Outstanding Player for that season and an exceptionally-talented rookie tailback straight from Sacramento State, Charles Roberts.

Then the talent, the bravado and a cocksure attitude all came together for one marvelous stretch of football through to the late fall. Winnipeg would reel off a club-record 12 consecutive victories, the third-longest win-streak in CFL history. But, with first place locked up at 14-2, the Bombers opted to rest some of their starters in the final two weeks (both losses) and by the time the playoffs rolled around their sharpness had been dulled considerably.

And it showed. Oh, how it showed.

The Bombers were sloppy in a 28-13 victory over the Ticats in the East Final and, against an 8-10 Stampeder team in the Grey Cup, before a sold-out crowd of 65,000-plus, were even worse. Winnipeg missed scoring opportunities, were atrocious in the secondary and gave up a punt-block for a touchdown while Westwood was just 1 for 4 in field goals in a 27-19 loss.

"Being a Christian man, I can't tell you how it really feels," said Bomber linebacker Antonio Armstrong in a somber dressing room afterward. "Words can't express how you feel when you lose after you put so much into something. You got guys in here who left their families behind. You got guys in here playing with aches and pains and they ain't supposed to be playing.... But they put it all on the line for the sake of the championship, for the Grey Cup. It's disgusting. Now we've got to go through the whole offseason with this in our minds."

"So what we had a winning season. 14-4...so what?" added Stegall. "Nobody looks at the regular season, they look at who is the Grey Cup champs. Who won it all. Calgary finished at 8-10, but they're the Grey Cup champs so nobody's going to remember their regular season record. "But when we get in this position next year, we'll definitely win."

All-everything receiver Milt Stegall: *Got Milt?*

Aye, but there's the rub—the Bombers would get close in 2002 and 2003, but couldn't even get back to the big dance to avenge their '01 disappointment in Montreal, despite two of the most memorable individual offensive performances in their 74 years.

By the start of '02—dubbed 'Unfinished Business'—the Bombers were already a famished bunch eager to get that elusive championship ring after a long drought. And from the opening kickoff of the season's lid-lifter there was an edge to Jones' game. He threw for five touchdowns in the first game and through the first handful of contests—four of them wins—he had already pitched for 19 scores. The Bombers finished 12-6 that season as Jones obliterated Dunigan's team record 36 touchdown passes by 10, just two shy of Flutie's CFL all-time best of 48. Stegall would latch on to 23 of those scoring strikes, establishing a new league standard for touchdowns while pulling in 106 passes for 1,896 yards en route to being named the CFL's Most Outstanding Player.

■ Blue Bomber brain trust, GM Brendan Taman and President Lyle Bauer, ponder how to improve the Blue Bombers in their 75th year.

Dave Darichuk

"Milt is the greatest player in this league," proclaimed Ritchie. "They ought to put him in the Hall of Fame now. I'm telling you, the guy is unbelievable."

The deal brought an end to Jones' highly successful run that was almost perfect except that he left without helping guide the team into the winner's circle.

But Stegall would be a non-factor when the real games began as he was injured in a regular-season finale victory over the Eskimos. The Bombers would not skip a beat without him in a 30-3 thrashing of the Lions in the West Semi, but he was sorely missed in Edmonton in the division final a week later. So, too, was steady receiver Robert Gordon (knee) and electrifying running back Charles Roberts who suffered a broken collar bone on his first carry against the Eskimos. Winnipeg would trail 32-6 before Jones rallied his troops—albeit in vain—in a 33-30 setback.

"What's scary is that we've had three years of pretty good football teams and we've got nothing to show for it," said Taman as the club picked up the pieces on another November disappointment. "I think it's only natural that you start to worry about whether that can continue, whether you can keep it going. Hopefully, we can, but a team is gauged by how many championships it has and, unfortunately, we have none."

The next season started well with a 4-0 start, the team's best in 16 years. But at year's end, Winnipeg fell to 11-7, behind the first-place Eskimos. That set up a showdown with the Riders, a team which had many of the same characteristics of the confident '01 Bombers, here in Winnipeg. Mind you, it was Troy Westwood who set the pre-game tone between the bitter rivals with this memorable quote—delivered with tongue firmly planted in his cheek, although many in Rider country to this day still find it offensive.

"I'd like to make an apology to the people of Saskatchewan," Westwood said. "Previous to this year's Labour Day game I made reference to the people of Saskatchewan as a bunch of 'banjo-pickin' inbreds.' I apologize for that statement and I was wrong to say such a thing. The vast majority of people from Saskatchewan have no idea how to play the banjo."

The quote may have been a classic, but the game was not. Already without five starters, the Bombers would lose Stegall early in the game with a hamstring pull. No matter. The Riders were clearly the superior side, building a 20-7 lead in the first half en route to a 37-21 win.

That defeat, the fourth consecutive bitterly disappointing end to a promising season, touched off a series of changes that would be felt well into the 2004 season. Before Christmas, offensive co-ordinator Paul LaPolice had been let go, Taman was promoted to GM while Ritchie had his director of football operations title stripped and was not offered a contract extension.

While the business side would continue its remarkable turnaround by whittling the debtload down to under $300,000 from $5.4 million, Ritchie's status—and the distraction it became early in the season—became the story and severely handcuffed a talented team.

The Bombers stumbled out of the gate in '04 at 2-5, continuing a downward trend that saw them lose 10 of 14 games dating back to midway through '03, before Ritchie was fired after 5 1/2 years on the job. Although he left with the third-most wins in Bomber history behind Bud Grant and Cal Murphy, Ritchie exited without that coveted Cup ring.

"We as a football team have been in a regression mode for quite some time," said Bauer upon making the announcement. "Sitting back and hoping that things would turn around is not acceptable. Hope is not a method. We have to make changes. We have to move forward because we are still committed to improving our football team and at this time we were digressing and not progressing.

"There's never good timing for a decision like this. We wanted to give Dave every opportunity to turn things around and make forward progress. But we've lost three games in a row here very, very handily. Staying status quo was not an option."

Dave Darichuk

■ Joe Fleming: *Brings big-time determination to the D-line.*

Jim Daley was promoted to head coach, but the drama of '04 would hardly screech to a stop there. Jones, who had been signed to a lucrative new deal on the eve of the season, struggled early and when his throwing shoulder lost its strength, surrendered his starting job to Kevin Glenn. It was Glenn's performance, coupled with the arrival of former Tennessee star Tee Martin from the NFL, that prompted Taman to make one of the biggest blockbuster trades in Bomber annals—dealing Jones and fullback Randy Bowles to Calgary for defensive tackle Joe Fleming, fullback Scott Regimbald and safety Wes Lysack.

The deal gave the Bombers the most feared defensive tackle duo in the CFL in Fleming and

Dave Darichuk

■ **Kevin Glenn:** *After much turmoil at the quarterback position, Kevin Glenn took the reins in 2005.*

Doug Brown, and brought an end to Jones' highly successful run that was almost perfect except that he left without helping guide the team into the winner's circle.

"No matter what I did, even in the years I was successful, there were murmurs," Jones said the day after the trade. "That I threw too many interceptions, even with all the touchdowns...My biggest thing is I'm proud of what we accomplished. Not only did we win football games, but we had a lot of fun. So, hopefully, I'm remembered like that. That's enough. Anything else is extra."

But while the Bombers hoped the trade would have a long-term impact the immediate results weren't there. Winnipeg struggled down the stretch, losing three of its last four, to finish 7-11 and miss the playoffs.

"The record itself was a concern even if we had been 7-11 and made the playoffs," said Taman. "The signs that were there weren't good. Had we beaten Edmonton and then snuck into the playoffs we still have the issues and concerns and winning would have just glossed that over...We've lost our swagger and we've got to get that back. We've got to look at everything and anything."

And so, as the Bombers prepared for their 75th season the same questions were lingering as in 1990. Can they find capable quarterbacking? Is Jim Daley the right man to get the Bombers back to the penthouse suite? And can this team which has often struggled just for survival wipe out its debt and at the same time capitalize on a dream by building a new state-of-the-art facility?

One thing is certain: we can pretty much guarantee the next 75 years will be just as riveting as the first. These are the Winnipeg Blue Bombers, after all, and the story of this football team has never been, and never will be, boring.

Winnipeg Free Press

■ **Head coach Jim Daley:** *Handed the difficult challenge of restoring the Bombers to their glory days.*

Dave Darichuk

■ **Punter Jon Ryan:** *One of the strongest legs in CFL history.*

ALL-TIME RECORDS

1930-2004

■ All-stars: Perry Tuttle, Tyrone Jones, James Murphy and Joe Poplawski.

WINNIPEG FOOTBALL CLUB MEMBERS IN THE CFL HALL OF FAME

1963 **Frank Hannibal** – Elected as a builder, Hannibal was Vice-President of the Winnipeg Football Club in 1934 and President in 1935 and '36. For nearly 30 years he served the Bombers and football in Western Canada.

Jack Jacobs – Elected as a player, Jacobs helped revolutionize the Canadian game with his special passing skills. During his relatively short Bomber career, he threw for 11,094 yards and 104 touchdowns in an era when running the ball was far more popular than passing it.

Eddie James – Elected as a player "Dynamite" Eddie James was considered one of the best players to ever come out of Western Canada. A native of Winnipeg, he was a colourful character who earned his nickname with a rare combination of power and speed. James played for both Winnipeg and Regina.

Fritz Hanson – Elected as a player, Hanson was one of the most electrifying players Canadian football fans had ever seen when he joined the Blue Bombers in the 1930s from his native North Dakota. His finest hour among many came in 1935 when he returned kicks for more than 300 yards leading the Blue Bombers to the West's first Grey Cup, and 18-12 win over the Hamilton Tigers.

Russ Rebholz – Elected as a player, Rebholz was one of the first imports to play football in Winnipeg. Nicknamed the "Wisconsin Wraith", Rebholz was considered a good all-round backfielder, and in an era when there was virtually no passing, he threw two touchdown passes in the 1935 Bombers' Grey Cup win.

1964 **Bert Warwick** – Elected as a builder, Warwick was head coach of the Bombers in 1945 and later served as chairman of the CFL rules committee during 50 years of being a leader and contributor to Canadian Football.

Tom Casey – Elected as a player, Tom "Citation" Casey was a two-way player who earned all-Western all-stars honours three times as a running back and three times as a defensive back during his six years with the Bombers from 1950 to 1955.

1966 **G. Sydney Halter** – Elected as a builder, Sir Sydney, as Jack Matheson of the *Tribune* called him, helped Joe Ryan and Frank Hannibal organize the Winnipeg Football Club in 1934. Halter became the first commissioner of the CFL when the Western Interprovincial Rugby Union and the Big Four amalgamated in 1958. He is also a member of Canada's Sports Hall of Fame.

Greg Kabat – Elected as a player, Kabat was another of the early American players to join the Winnipeg Football Club. He played quarterback, guard, fullback, flying wing and also did some place-kicking as he helped lead Winnipeg to the 1935 Grey Cup victory.

1967 **Carl Cronin** – Elected as a player, Cronin was the first import player recruited by the "Winnipegs" in 1932 out of Notre Dame. He was a backfielder, kicker and hard-hitting linebacker who served as an inspiration to those around him. As a playing coach in 1933, he led Winnipeg to the Western Canadian title.

1968 **Joe B. Ryan** – Elected as a builder, he engineered the amalgamation of the Winnpeg Rugby Club and St. John's in the early 1930s, paving the way to Winnipeg's first Grey Cup win in 1935. Ryan was the Manager of the club in 1935 and was credited with recruiting Fritz Hanson, Bud Marquardt and Herb Peschel, among others.

1970 **Art Chipman** – Elected as a builder, Arthur Chipman was credited with helping save the game during the

■ Jack Jacobs

Second World War years in the West. He was President of the Blue Bombers from 1944 to 1948 and also served as President of the Western Rugby Union and the Canadian Rugby Union.

Art Stevenson – Elected as a player, Art starred for the Bombers in the late 1930s and early 1940s. He was a quarterback and halfback, plus an accomplished kicker, who scored the winning point in Winnipeg's 1939 Grey Cup win over Ottawa.

1973 Leo Lewis – Elected as a player, the Lincoln Locomotive joined the Bombers in 1955. During his 11 years, he made six all-star teams, rushed for 8,861 yards with a 6.6 yard average and also posted a phenomenal 29.1 yard average on kickoff returns. Bud Grant called Lewis the greatest player he ever coached.

1974 Les Lear – Elected as a player, Lear was the first Canadian developed player to go to the NFL where he played guard with Cleveland, the L.A. Rams and Detroit. He helped the Bombers win the 1939 and 1941 Grey Cup games.

Andy Currie – Elected as a builder, Andrew Currie was also a terrific player for both the Blue Bombers and Regina in the late 1920s and early 1930s. After his playing days, Andy coached high school football before getting heavily involved in officiating. He was responsible for revising and rewriting the rule book which was adopted by the CFL in 1967.

1975 Ken Ploen – Elected as a player, one of Ploen's most unique claims to fame was that he played in both the Rose Bowl and the Grey Cup game in 1957. Earning all-star honours as both a quarterback and defensive back during his 11 years with the Bombers, Ploen was considered one of the integral parts of the Bombers four Grey Cup victories in the 50s and 60s.

1976 Ches McCance – Elected as a player, McCance was a two-way end who earned all-Western all-star honours in 1940 and 1941. He helped the Bombers win the 1939 and 1941 Grey Cup games.

1981 Gerry James – Elected as a player, James was the son of "Dynamite" Eddie James, and was naturally nicknamed "Kid Dynamite." He joined the Bombers as a 17-year old running back and was the first ever winner of the Schenley Award as Top Canadian in the CFL in 1954. He won that award again in 1957 and combined his football career with several seasons in the NHL.

■ Dynamite and the Kid: *Eddie James with son Gerry*

1982 Buddy Tinsley – Elected as a player, Robert Porter Tinsley spent 11 seasons with the Bombers, playing both ways at tackle on the offensive and defensive lines. Tinsley joined the Bombers from the Los Angeles Dons of the All-American Conference after starring at Baylor University in Texas. He was an eight-time all-Western all-star, five times on the offensive line.

1983 Herb Gray – Elected as a player, Herb Gray played on both sides of the ball but was best known as a ferocious hard-hitting defensive lineman. He made seven Western Conference all-star teams, one as an offensive guard, the other six as a defensive end. Part of the great teams of the Bud Grant era, Herb Gray was the first defensive player in 1960 to win the Schenley Most Outstanding Lineman award.

Bud Grant – Elected as a builder, Harry Peter Bud Grant was also an outstanding player for the Blue Bombers, making three Western all-star teams as an offensive end. He went straight from playing to coaching, leading the Blue Bombers to six Grey Cup games, four of which they won. He left Winnipeg to become head coach of the Minnesota Vikings in 1967.

Earl Lunsford – Elected as a player, the man known as the "Earthquake" was an outstanding fullback for the Calgary Stampeders, becoming the first player in pro football history to rush for a mile in one season when he ran for 1794 yards in 1961. Lunsford was General Manager of the Blue Bombers from 1968 to 1982, enjoying many successes on and off the field.

1984 Frank Rigney – Elected as a player, "Rigs" as he was known was simply one of the best offensive linemen in Blue Bombers and CFL history. He anchored Winnipeg's offensive line from 1958 to 1967, earning seven western all-star nominations, three all-Canadian awards, and recognition as the top lineman in the league in 1961.

1985 John Helton – Elected as a player, Helton played the bulk of his sensational career in Calgary before joining the Bombers for his final four seasons from 1979 to 1982. Helton made 12 division all-star teams, he was a nine-time All Canadian. Twice he was named the Schenley Most Outstanding Defensive Player in the CFL.

1987 – Dick Huffman – Elected as a player, Huffman played five of his CFL seasons with the Bombers from 1951-55 before joining Calgary. He joined the Bombers from the Los Angeles Rams at a time when Canadian Football League teams paid their imports as much as the NFL, sometimes more. He played both ways, but was best known for his work as a defensive lineman. Huffman made eight Western all-star teams, five with the Bombers.

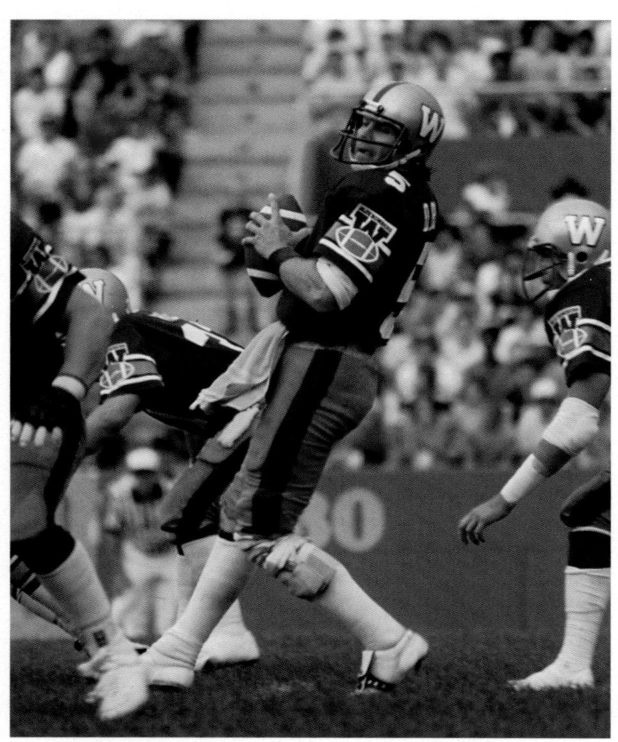

■ Dieter Brock

1989 Karl Slocomb – Elected as a builder, Slocomb served tirelessly on the Bomber executive for many years before becoming President of the club in 1953. He went to the presidency of the Western Interprovincial Football Union and took over as President of the Canadian Rugby Union in 1960.

1994 Tom Clements – Elected as a player, Tom went straight from Notre Dame to the Ottawa Rough Riders in 1975. He then spent time in Saskatchewan, Hamilton and the NFL before being acquired by the Blue Bombers in a trade with Hamilton in 1983. He helped the Bombers end a 22-year Grey Cup drought in 1984, and finished his career with 39,041 yards passing. In addition to being Rookie-of-the-Year in 1975, he was named the CFL's Most Outstanding Player while with the Bombers in 1987.

Tommy Grant – Elected as a player, Grant only played one year with the Bombers, that was in 1969. Otherwise, he had many great years as a receiver in Hamilton, appearing in nine Grey Cups and winning four of them.

1995 Dieter Brock – Elected as a player, Brock, a.k.a. "Dieter" and "The Birmingham Rifle" was one of the finest pure passers in CFL history. He is the only player in Blue Bombers history to win back-to-back Most Outstanding Player awards in 1980 and '81. During his decade with the Bombers, he did everything but bring the Grey Cup back to Winnipeg.

1998 Joe Poplawski – Elected as a player, "Joe Pop" is another one of the all-time great Blue Bombers. In a relatively short nine-year career on 1978 to 1986, Poplawski was named rookie of the year, won two other Schenley Awards as best Canadian in the CFL, and was named to the All-Canadian team five times. Poplawski caught 549 passes for 8341 yards before retiring at the tender age of 29.

2000 James Murphy – Elected as a player, "Murph" joined the Bombers in 1982 and went on to play eight superb seasons. He was named the CFL's Most Outstanding Player in 1986, he earned three Grey Cup rings, and he finished his career with 573 catches for 9036 yards.

2001 Bill Frank – Elected as a player, Frank played with the Blue Bombers from 1970 to 1976 after starting his long and glorious CFL career with B.C. in 1962. He was named to seven All-Canadian teams, and was a key player in helping turn the Bombers around after the difficult times of the late 1960s.

2002 **Paul Bennett** – Elected as a player, "Benny" played four of his 11 CFL seasons with the Blue Bombers after starting off with the Argos. From 1983 to 1986, he was an outstanding safety and punt returner for the Bombers, earning the league's Most Outstanding Canadian Award in 1983.

Less Browne – Elected as a player, the CFL's all-time interception leader played just three years of his long and productive career with the Bombers. But, from 1989 to 1991, he patrolled the corner in the Bombers secondary with the same efficiency he had shown during his many All-Canadian seasons, and helped the Bombers win the 1990 Grey Cup.

2003 **Chris Walby** – Elected as a player, Walby is considered to be among the greatest offensive linemen in CFL history. A Winnipeg native, he helped the Bombers in three Grey Cup Championships during his career which spanned 1981 to 1996. Twice he was named the CFL's Top Offensive Lineman, and nine times he made the All-Canadian team.

2004 **Cal Murphy** – Elected as a builder, Murphy became the Blue Bombers head coach in 1983 and went on to become both coach and manager of the Bombers, until 1996. His teams were loaded with talent, were perennial contenders, and three times they brought the Grey Cup back to Winnipeg. The Cal Murphy era was one of the more memorable in Blue Bombers history.

WINNIPEG FOOTBALL CLUB HALL OF FAME

1984

Builders

Arthur Chipman
H.P. "Bud" Grant
G. Sydney Halter
A.H. "Bert" Warwick
Andrew Currie
Frank Hannibal
Joseph "Joe" B. Ryan

Players

Lou Adelman
Carl Cronin
Fritz Hanson
Gerry James
Greg Kabat
Leo Lewis
Chester McCance
Jeff Nicklin
Ken Ploen
Karl Slocomb
"Bud" Tinsley
Tom Casey
Herbert "Herb" Gray
Jack Jacobs
Eddie James
Les Lear
Bud Marquardt
Lou Mogul
Robert Porter
Russ Rebholz
Art Stevenson

1985

Builders

Barry Bain
Ralph Misener
Jim Russell
Gordon Lawson
Ralph Parliament

Players

Andy Bieber
Martin Gainor
Bill Nairn
Frank Rigney
Cliff Roseborough
Bill Cerretti
Dick Huffman
Steve Patrick
Bob Sandberg
Mel Wilson

1986

Builders

Gordon Gage
Reg Threlfall

Players

Farrell Funston
Cornel Piper
Gordon Rowland
Ed Kotowich
Ernie Pitts

1987

Builders

Dr. Neville Winograd

Players

Ken Nielsen
Norm Rauhaus
Herb Peschel
Roger Savoie

1988

Builders

Karl Wintermute

Players

Jack Delveaux
Phil Minnick
Tom Lumsden
Dick Thornton

1989

Builders

Cedric Gyles

Players

Dave Burkholder
Don Jonas
Henry Janzen
Dave Raimey

1990

Builders

Earl Lunsford

Players

Dieter Brock
Joe Poplawski
Bill Frank

1991

Builders

Paul Robson

Players

John Bonk — George Druxman
Bob Swift

1992

Builders

Art Tooley

Players

Nick Bastaja — Tom Clements
Charlie Shepard

1993

Builders

Paul Quinton

Players

Paul Bennett — Willard Reaves
Ed Ulmer

1994

Builders

Gordon Mackie

Players

Ron "Pepe" Latourelle — Haywood "Butch" Norman
Jim "Jay" Washington

1995

Builders

John Michaels — Ross Smith

Players

Rick House — James Murphy

1996

Builders

Leland S. "Tote" Mitchell

Players

Rod Hill — Bud Korchak
Nick Miller

1997

Builders

Art Ceretti

Players

Ken Hailey — Perry Tuttle
James West

1998

Builders

Dr. Jan Brown — Sam Diamond

Players

Lyle Bauer — Trevor Kennerd

1999

Builders

William Culver Riley

Players

Jeff Boyd — Tyrone Jones

2000

Builders

Earl Hiebert

Players

Stan Mikawos — Chris Walby
Bill Whisler

2001

Builders

Vickie Czarnecki — Ken Davey

Players

Greg Battle — Sherwyn Thorson
Gerald Wilcox

2002

Builders

Barry Manning — Cal Murphy

Players

Mike Holmes — Paul Randolph

2003

Builders

Harvey Scrivener

Players

Matt Dunigan — Bob Cameron

2004

Builders

Ken Houssin

Players

Darryl Sampson — Dave Black

Dave Darichuk

■ Safety Wes Lysak – 2005.

WINNIPEG BLUE BOMBERS IN THE GREY CUP

GREY CUP WINS/APPEARANCES: (10/24)	
Winnipeg Football Club (1/1):	1935
Winnipeg RCAF Bombers (0/2):	1942, 1943
Winnipeg Blue Bombers (9/21):	1937, 1938, 1939, 1941, 1945, 1946, 1947, 1950, 1953, 1957, 1958, 1959, 1961, 1962, 1965, 1984, 1988, 1990, 1992, 1993, 2001

YEAR	DATE	SITE	WINNER		LOSER	
2001	Nov. 25	Montréal	Calgary Stampeders	27	Winnipeg Blue Bombers	19
1993	Nov. 28	Calgary	Edmonton Eskimos	33	Winnipeg Blue Bombers	23
1992	Nov. 29	Toronto	Calgary Stampeders	24	Winnipeg Blue Bombers	10
1990	Nov. 25	Vancouver	Winnipeg Blue Bombers	50	Edmonton Eskimos	11
1988	Nov. 27	Ottawa	Winnipeg Blue Bombers	22	B.C. Lions	21
1984	Nov. 18	Edmonton	Winnipeg Blue Bombers	47	Hamilton Tiger-Cats	17
1965	Nov. 27	Toronto	Hamilton Tiger-Cats	22	Winnipeg Blue Bombers	16
1962	Dec. 1-2*	Toronto	Winnipeg Blue Bombers	28	Hamilton Tiger-Cats	27
1961	Dec. 2**	Toronto	Winnipeg Blue Bombers	21	Hamilton Tiger-Cats	14
1959	Nov. 28	Toronto	Winnipeg Blue Bombers	21	Hamilton Tiger-Cats	7
1958	Nov. 29	Vancouver	Winnipeg Blue Bombers	35	Hamilton Tiger-Cats	28
1957	Nov. 30	Toronto	Hamilton Tiger-Cats	32	Winnipeg Blue Bombers	7
1953	Nov. 28	Toronto	Hamilton Tiger-Cats	12	Winnipeg Blue Bombers	6
1950	Nov. 25	Toronto	Toronto Argonauts	13	Winnipeg Blue Bombers	0
1947	Nov. 27	Toronto	Toronto Argonauts	10	Winnipeg Blue Bombers	9
1946	Nov. 30	Toronto	Toronto Argonauts	28	Winnipeg Blue Bombers	6
1945	Dec. 1	Toronto	Toronto Argonauts	35	Winnipeg Blue Bombers	0
1943	Nov. 27	Toronto	Hamilton Flying Wildcats	23	Winnipeg RCAF Bombers	14
1942	Dec. 5	Toronto	Toronto RCAF	8	Winnipeg RCAF Bombers	5
1941	Nov. 29	Toronto	Winnipeg Blue Bombers	18	Ottawa Rough Riders	16
1939	Dec. 9	Ottawa	Winnipeg Blue Bombers	8	Ottawa Rough Riders	7
1938	Dec. 10	Toronto	Toronto Argonauts	30	Winnipeg Blue Bombers	7
1937	Dec. 11	Toronto	Toronto Argonauts	4	Winnipeg Blue Bombers	3
1935	Dec. 7	Hamilton	Winnipeg Football Club	18	Hamilton Tigers	12

*Fog halted Grey Cup. Final 9:29 of fourth quarter was played on December 2, 1962.

**Final decided in overtime.

RECORD VERSUS OPPONENTS	GP	W	L	F	A
vs. HAMILTON based Teams	10	6	4	213	194
vs. TORONTO based Teams	7	0	7	30	128
vs. OTTAWA based Teams	2	2	0	26	23
vs. EDMONTON based Teams	2	1	1	73	44
vs. CALGARY based Teams	2	0	2	29	43
vs. B.C. based Teams	1	1	0	22	21

WINNIPEG BLUE BOMBERS PLAYOFF RECORD

Year	Round	Date	Opponent	Score	Result
1933					
	WS	Nov. 4	vs Regina	11 - 1	W
	WF	Nov. 11	vs Calgary	15 - 1	W
	GCS	Dec. 2	@ Toronto	13 - 0	L
1934					
	WS	Nov. 3	@ Regina	8 - 0	L
1935					
	WS	Nov. 2	vs Regina	13 - 6	W
	WF	Nov. 9	vs Calgary	7 - 0	W
	WF	Dec. 2	@ Ass. Coll.	17 - 0	W
1936					
	WS	Oct. 24	@ Regina	7 - 4	W
	WS	Oct. 31	vs Regina	20 - 5	L
1937					
	WF	Nov. 6	vs Calgary	13 - 10	L
	WF	Nov. 11	@ Calgary	9 - 1	W
1938					
	WS	Oct. 29	vs Regina	13 - 0	W
	WF	Nov. 5	@ Calgary	12 - 7	W
	WF	Nov. 12	vs Calgary	13 - 2	W
1939					
	WF	Nov. 11	vs Calgary	13 - 7	L
	WF	Nov. 18	@ Calgary	28 - 7	W
1940					
	WF	Nov. 2	@ Calgary	7 - 0	W
	WF	Nov. 9	vs Calgary	23 - 2	W
1941					
	WF	Nov. 8	@ Regina	8 - 6	L
	WF	Nov. 11	vs Regina	18 - 12	W
	WF	Nov. 15	vs Regina	8 - 2	W
1942					
	WF	Oct. 31	vs RCAF Flyers	18 - 14	L
	WF	Nov. 3	vs RCAF Flyers	20 - 11	W
1943					
	WF	Nov. 6	vs Regina	1 - 0	W
	WF	Nov. 11	@ Regina	11 - 0	W
1945					
	WF	Nov. 10	vs Calgary	9 - 6	W
1946					
	WF	Oct. 26	@ Calgary	21 - 18	L
	WF	Nov. 2	vs Calgary	12 - 0	W
1947					
	WF	Nov. 1	vs Calgary	16 - 4	W
	WF	Nov. 11	@ Calgary	15 - 3	L
	WF	Nov. 15	vs Calgary	10 - 3	W
1950					
	WF	Nov. 4	vs Edmonton	17 - 16	L
	WF	Nov.11	@ Edmonton	22 - 12	W
	WF	Nov.13	@ Edmonton	29 - 6	W

Year	Round	Date	Opponent	Score	Result
1951					
	WS	Oct. 27	@ Edmonton	4 - 1	L
1952					
	WF	Nov. 1	@ Edmonton	28 - 12	W
	WF	Nov. 8	vs Edmonton	18 - 12	L
	WF	Nov. 11	vs Edmonton	22 - 11	L
1953					
	WS	Oct. 28	@ Saskatchewan	43 - 5	W
	WS	Oct. 31	vs Saskatchewan	18 - 17	L
	WF	Nov. 7	vs Edmonton	25 - 7	L
	WF	Nov. 11	@ Edmonton	21 - 17	W
	WF	Nov. 14	@ Edmonton	30 - 24	W
	GCS	Nov. 21	vs Toronto Balmy Beach	24 - 3	W
1954					
	WS	Oct. 30	@ Saskatchewan	14 - 14	T
	WS	Nov. 1	@ Saskatchewan	13 - 11	W
	WF	Nov. 6	@ Edmonton	9 - 3	L
	WF	Nov. 11	vs Edmonton	12 - 6	W
	WF	Nov. 13	@ Edmonton	10 - 5	L
1955					
	WS	Nov. 5	@ Saskatchewan	16 - 7	W
	WS	Nov. 7	vs Saskatchewan	9 - 8	L
	WF	Nov. 11	vs Edmonton	29 - 6	L
	WF	Nov. 16	@ Edmonton	26 - 6	L
1956					
	WS	Nov. 3	@ Saskatchewan	42 - 7	L
	WS	Nov. 5	vs Saskatchewan	19 - 8	W
1957					
	WS	Nov. 9	vs Calgary	13 - 13	T
	WS	Nov. 11	@ Calgary	15 - 3	W
	WF	Nov. 16	vs Edmonton	19 - 7	W
	WF	Nov. 20	@ Edmonton	5 - 4	L
	WF	Nov. 23	@ Edmonton	17 - 2	W
1958					
	WF	Nov. 15	@ Edmonton	30 - 7	W
	WF	Nov. 19	vs Edmonton	30 - 7	L
	WF	Nov. 22	vs Edmonton	23 - 7	W
1959					
	WF	Nov. 11	@ Edmonton	19 - 11	W
	WF	Nov. 14	vs Edmonton	16 - 8	W
1960					
	WF	Nov. 12	@ Edmonton	22 - 16	W
	WF	Nov. 14	vs Edmonton	10 - 5	L
	WF	Nov. 19	vs Edmonton	4 - 2	L
1961					
	WF	Nov. 18	@ Calgary	14 - 1	W
	WF	Nov. 22	vs Calgary	43 - 14	W

Year	Round	Date	Opponent	Score	Result
1962					
	WF	Nov. 17	@ Calgary	20 - 14	L
	WF	Nov. 21	vs Calgary	19 - 11	W
	WF	Nov. 24	vs Calgary	12 - 7	W
1965					
	WS	Nov. 7	vs Saskatchewan	15 - 9	W
	WF	Nov. 13	@ Calgary	27 - 9	L
	WF	Nov. 17	vs Calgary	15 - 11	W
	WF	Nov. 20	@ Calgary	19 - 12	W
1966					
	WF	Nov. 6	vs Edmonton	16 - 8	W
	WF	Nov. 13	@ Saskatchewan	14 - 7	L
	WF	Nov. 19	vs Saskatchewan	21 - 19	L
1971					
	WF	Nov. 6	@ Saskatchewan	34 - 23	L
1972					
	WF	Nov. 19	vs Saskatchewan	27 - 24	L
1975					
	WS	Nov. 8	@ Saskatchewan	42 - 24	L
1976					
	WS	Nov. 14	@ Edmonton	14 - 12	L
1977					
	WS	Nov. 12	@ B.C.	33 - 32	L
1978					
	WS	Nov. 12	@ Calgary	38 - 4	L
1980					
	WS	Nov. 9	vs Calgary	32 - 14	W
	WF	Nov. 15	@ Edmonton	34 - 24	L
1981					
	WS	Nov. 8	vs B.C.	15 - 11	L
1982					
	WS	Nov. 14	vs Calgary	24 - 3	W
	WF	Nov. 21	@ Edmonton	24 - 21	L
1983					
	WS	Nov. 13	vs Edmonton	49 - 22	W
	WF	Nov. 20	@ B.C.	39 - 21	L
1984					
	WS	Nov. 4	@ Edmonton	55 - 20	W
	WF	Nov. 11	@ B.C.	31 - 14	W
1985					
	WS	Nov. 10	vs Edmonton	22 - 15	W
	WF	Nov. 17	@ B.C.	42 - 22	L
1986					
	WS	Nov. 15	@ B.C.	21 - 14	L
1987					
	EF	Nov. 22	vs Toronto	19 - 3	L
1988					
	ES	Nov. 13	vs Hamilton	35 - 28	W
	EF	Nov. 20	@ Toronto	27 - 11	W
1989					
	ES	Nov. 12	@ Toronto	30 - 7	W
	EF	Nov. 19	@ Hamilton	14 - 10	L
1990					
	EF	Nov. 18	vs Toronto	20 - 17	W
1991					
	ES	Nov. 10	vs Ottawa	26 - 8	W
	EF	Nov. 17	@ Toronto	42 - 3	L
1992					
	EF	Nov. 22	vs Hamilton	59 - 11	W
1993					
	EF	Nov. 21	vs Hamilton	20 - 19	W
1994					
	ES	Nov. 13	vs Ottawa	26 - 16	W
	EF	Nov. 20	vs Baltimore	14 - 12	L
1995					
	SSF	Nov. 4	@ Baltimore	36 - 21	L
1996					
	WS	Nov. 10	@ Edmonton	68 - 7	L
2000					
	ES	Nov. 12	@ Hamilton	22 - 20	W
	EF	Nov. 19	@ Montreal	35 - 24	L
2001					
	EF	Nov. 18	vs Hamilton	28 - 13	W
2002					
	WS	Nov. 10	vs B.C.	30 - 3	W
	WF	Nov. 17	@ Edmonton	33 - 30	L
2003					
	WS	Nov. 2	vs. Saskatchewan	37 - 21	L

Legend: WS - West Semifinal; WF - West Final; ES - East Semifinal; EF - East Final; SSF - South Semifinal; GCS - Grey Cup Semifinal

Dave Darichuk

■ Kick returner/receiver Keith Stokes – 2005.

WINNIPEG FOOTBALL CLUB THROUGHOUT THE YEARS

YEAR	PRESIDENT	MANAGER	COACH	W	L	T	PLACE
1930	Dick Mahoney	Tote Mitchell	Fred Ritter	0	4	0	2nd
1931	Dick Mahoney	Joe Ryan	Pete Barnes	1	3	0	
			& Jack Millidge				2nd
1932	Leo McCarth	Joe Ryan	Carl Cronin	2	3	1	2nd
1933	Barry Bain	Joe Ryan	Carl Cronin	2	0	0	1st
1934	Barry Bain	Committee	Greg Kabat	2	0	0	1st
1935	Frank Hannibal	Joe Ryan	Bob Fritz	3	0	0	1st
1936	Frank Hannibal	Frank Emma	Bob Fritz	5	2	1	1st
1937	Les Isard	Lou Adelmon	Bob Fritz	4	4	0	2nd
1938	Les Isard	Lou Adelmon	Reg Threlfall	6	2	0	2nd
1939	Wally Brown	Joe Ryan	Reg Threlfall	10	2	0	1st
1940	Wally Brown	Joe Ryan	Reg Threlfall	6	2	0	1st
1941	Frank Hannibal	Joe Ryan	Reg Threlfall	6	2	0	1st
1942	Sid Halter	Bill Cockburn	Reg Threlfall	—	—	—	—
1943	Bert Longstaff	Bill Cockburn	Reg Threlfall	—	—	—	—
1944	Art Chipman	NO TEAM	—	—	—	—	—
1945	Art Chipman	LouAdelmon	Bert Warwick	—	—	—	—
1946	Art Chipman	Scott Kennedy	Jack West	5	3	0	2nd
1947	Art Chipman	GordonBieber	Jack West	5	3	0	1st
1948	Eddie Armstrong	Scott Kennedy	Jack West	3	9	0	3rd
1949	Eddie Armstrong	Scott Kennedy	Frank Larson	2	12	0	4th
1950	Ralph Misener	Scott Kennedy	Frank Larson	10	4	0	1st
1951	Ralph Misener	Scott Kennedy	George Trafton	8	6	0	3rd
1952	Culver Riley	Scott Kennedy	George Trafton	12	3	1	1st
1953	Karl Slocomb	Scott Kennedy	George Trafton	8	8	0	3rd
1954	Ralph Misener	Bill Boivin	Al Sherman	8	6	2	3rd
1955	Ralph Misener	Bill Boivin	Al Sherman	7	9	0	3rd
1956	Jim Russell	Bill Boivin	Al Sherman	9	7	0	3rd
1957	Jim Russell	Bill Boivin	Bud Grant	12	4	0	2nd
1958	Ralph Parliament	Jim Ausley	Bud Grant	13	3	0	1st
1959	Ralph Parliament	Jim Ausley	Bud Grant	12	4	0	1st
1960	Gordon Lawson	Jim Ausley	Bud Grant	14	2	0	1st
1961	Gordon Lawson	Jim Ausley	Bud Grant	13	3	0	1st
1962	Karl Wintermute	Jim Ausley	Bud Grant	11	5	0	1st
1963	Karl Wintermute	Jim Ausley	Bud Grant	7	9	0	4th
1964	Neville Winograd	Bud Grant	Bud Grant	1	14	1	5th
1965	Neville Winograd	Bud Grant	Bud Grant	10	6	0	2nd
1966	Don Tomlin	Bud Grant	Bud Grant	8	7	1	2nd
1967	Don Tomlin	Terry Hind	Joe Zaleski	4	12	0	4th
1968	Ced Gyles	Earl Lunsford	Joe Zaleski	3	13	0	5th
1969	Ced Gyles	Earl Lunsford	Joe Zaleski	3	12	1	5th
1970	Paul Quinton	Earl Lunsford	Jim Spavital	2	14	0	5th
1971	Paul Quinton	Earl Lunsford	Jim Spavital	7	8	1	3rd
1972	Gordon Muirhead	Earl Lunsford	Jim Spavital	10	6	0	1 st
1973	Gordon Muirhead	Earl Lunsford	Jim Spavital	4	11	1	5th
1974	Paul Morton	Earl Lunsford	Bud Riley	8	8	0	4th
1975	Paul Morton	Earl Lunsford	Bud Riley	6	8	2	3rd
1976	Earle Hiebert	Earl Lunsford	Bud Riley	10	6	0	3rd
1977	Earle Hiebert	Earl Lunsford	Bud Riley	10	6	0	3rd
1978	Ross Smith	Earl Lunsford	Ray Jauch	9	7	0	3rd

YEAR	PRESIDENT	MANAGER	COACH	W	L	T	PLACE
1979	Ross Smith	Earl Lunsford	Ray Jauch	4	12	0	4th
1980	Joe Wilder	Earl Lunsford	Ray Jauch	10	6	0	2nd
1981	Joe Wilder	Earl Lunsford	Ray Jauch	11	5	0	2nd
1982	George Graham	Earl Lunsford	RayJauch	11	5	0	2nd
1983	George Graham	Paul Robson	CalMurphy	9	7	0	2nd
1984	Jan Brown	Paul Robson	Cal Murphy	11	4	1	2nd
1985	Jan Brown	Paul Robson	Cal Murphy	12	4	0	2nd
1986	Ken Matchett	Paul Robson	Cal Murphy	11	7	0	3rd
1987	Ken Matchett	Cal Murphy	Mike Riley	13	5	0	1st
1988	Ross Brown	Cal Murphy	Mike Riley	9	9	0	2nd
1989	Ross Brown	Cal Murphy	Mike Riley	7	11	0	3rd
1990	Ted Bartman	Cal Murphy	Mike Riley	12	6	0	1st
1991	Ted Bartman	Cal Murphy	Darryl Rogers	9	9	0	2nd
1992	Bruce Robinson	Cal Murphy	Urban Bowman*	11	7	0	1st
1993	Bruce Robinson	Cal Murphy	Cal Murphy	14	4	0	1st
1994	Reg Low	Cal Murphy	Cal Murphy	13	5	0	1st
1995	Reg Low	Cal Murphy	Cal Murphy	7	11	0	5th
1996	Lynn Bishop	Don Cozine	Cal Murphy	9	9	0	3rd
1997	Lynn Bishop	Ken Bishop	Jeff Reinebold	4	14	0	3rd
1998	Don Bryk	Ken Bishop	Jeff Reinebold	2	12	0	
			Gary Hoffman	1	3	0	4th
1999	Bob Miles	Ken Bishop	Dave Ritchie	6	12	0	4th
2000	Bob Miles	Lyle Bauer	Dave Ritchie	7	10	1	3rd
2001	Lyle Bauer	Lyle Bauer	Dave Ritchie	14	4	0	1st
2002	Lyle Bauer	Lyle Bauer	Dave Ritchie	12	6	0	2nd
2003	Lyle Bauer	Lyle Bauer	Dave Ritchie	11	7	0	2nd
2004	Lyle Bauer	Brendan Taman	Dave Ritchie	2	5	0	
			Jim Daley	5	6	0	4th

**Served as head coach for Cal Murphy while he was recuperating from heart transplant.*

Dave Darichuk

■ **Defensive lineman Doug Brown - 2005.**

CFL ALL-STARS

1962	
Herb Gray	DE
Leo Lewis	RB
Frank Rigney	OT
Gord Rowland	LB

1963	
Dick Thornton	DB

1965	
Ken Ploen	QB
Frank Rigney	OT
Dick Thornton	

1966	
Phil Minnick	LB
Dave Raimey	RB
Frank Rigney	OT
Ed Ulmer	DB

1967	
Bill Frank	OT

1968	
Ken Nielsen	FL

1969	
Phil Minnick	LB
Ken Nielsen	FL

1970	
Bill Frank	OT

1971	
Bill Frank	OT
Don Jonas	QB
Bob LaRose	WR
Bob Swift	C
Jim Thorpe	SE

1972	
Grady Cavness	DB
Bill Frank	OT
Mack Herron	RB
Don Jonas	QB
Bob Lueck	OG
Bob Swift	C

1973	
Bill Frank	OT

1974	
Bob Swift	C
Paul Williams	DB

1976	
Brian Herosian	DB
Butch Norman	OT
Harry Walters	MLB
Jim Washington	RB

1977	
Tom Scott	SB
Jim Washington	RB

1978	
Joe Poplawski	WR

1979	
John Helton	DT

1980	
Dieter Brock	QB
Larry Butler	OG
Mike Holmes	WR
William Miller	RB
Butch Norman	OT

1981	
Dieter Brock	QB
Larry Butler	OG
Trevor Kennerd	K
Joe Poplawski	SB

1982	
John Bonk	C
Pete Catan	DE
John Helton	DT
William Miller	RB
Vince Phason	DB
Bobby Thompson	OT

1983	
Paul Bennett	DB
John Bonk	C

1984	
Nick Bastaja	OG
John Bonk	C
Aaron Brown	MLB
Tom Clements	QB
Ken Hailey	DB
Tyrone Jones	OLB
Joe Poplawski	SB
Willard Reaves	RB
David Shaw	DB
Chris Walby	OT

1985	
Nick Bastaja	OG
John Bonk	C
Jeff Boyd	WR
Ken Hailey	DB
Tyrone Jones	OLB
Trevor Kennerd	K
Joe Poplawski	SB
Willard Reaves	RB
Chris Walby	OT

1986	
Roy Bennett	CB
Scott Flagel	S
Tyrone Jones	OLB
James Murphy	WR
Joe Poplawski	SB
Chris Walby	OT

1987	
Roy Bennett	CB
Tom Clements	QB
Scott Flagel	S
Ken Hailey	DB
James Jefferson	CB
Tyrone Jones	OLB
Willard Reaves	RB
Perry Tuttle	SB
Chris Walby	OT
James West	MLB

1988	
Bob Cameron	P
James Murphy	WR
Bennie Thompson	S

1989	
Bob Cameron	P
Rod Hill	CB
Chris Walby	OT

1990	
Greg Battle	LB
Less Browne	CB
Bob Cameron	P
Rod Hill	CB
Robert Mimbs	RB
Chris Walby	OT

1991	
Greg Battle	LB
Less Browne	CB
Robert Mimbs	RB
Chris Walby	OT

1992	
Michael Richardson	RB
Troy Westwood	K

1993	
David Black	OG
Bob Cameron	P
Elfrid Payton	LB
Michael Richardson	RB
Darryl Sampson	DB
Chris Walby	OT
David Williams	WR

1994	
Chris Walby	OT
Gerald Wilcox	SB

1996	
K.D. Williams	LB

1997	
Shon'te Peoples	LB
Milt Stegall	WR

1998	
Eric Blount	ST
Joe Fleming	DT

1999	
Maurice Kelly	LB

2000	
Albert Johnson III	ST
Milt Stegall	SB

2001	
Juran Bolden	CB
Doug Brown	DT
Khari Jones	QB
Brett MacNeil	OG
Dave Mudge	OT
Harold Nash, Jr.	DB
Charles Roberts	ST
Milt Stegall	SB

2002	
Doug Brown	DT
Denny Fortney	DT
Dave Mudge	OT
Charles Roberts	RB
Milt Stegall	SB

2003	
Daved Benefield	DE
Charles Roberts	RB

2004	
Charles Roberts	RB
Keith Stokes	ST

GREY CUP WINNING TEAM ROSTERS

WINNIPEG RUGBY FOOTBALL CLUB 1935 GREY CUP CHAMPIONS

WINNIPEG BLUE BOMBERS 1939 GREY CUP CHAMPIONS

FRONT ROW L. to R.: Wayne Sheeley, Mel Wilson, Ches McCance, Herb Peschel, Bill Ceretti, Art Stevenson, Greg Kabat, Martin Gainor, Ed Kushner, Les Lear, Bill Nairn, Cliff Rosborough, Lou Mogul, Fritz Hansen.

BACK ROW L. TO R.: Herb Mobberley, Jack Manners, Carl Krisko, Andy Bieber, Bill Boivin, John Lake, Ben Hatskin, Hal Davidson, Al Waycock, Harry Badger, Frank Mulvey, Jeff Nicklin, Bud Marquardt, Martin Platz, Bert Iannone.

WINNIPEG BLUE BOMBERS 1941 GREY CUP CHAMPIONS

The only known photograph of the 1941 Grey Cup team. The players included: Nate Shore, Mel Wilson, Ken Draper, Lou Mogul, Cliff Roseborough, Bill Boivin, Alex Lindsay, Ben Hatskin, Herb Peschel, Duke Manners, Art Kolisnyk, Bud Marquardt, Kippy McFadyen, Lloyd Evenson, Wayne Sheley, Les Lear, Jim Lander, Chick Chikowski, Wilf Daniels, Ches McCance, Bernie Thornton, Rube Ludwig, Fritz Hanson, Ken Preston.

WINNIPEG BLUE BOMBERS 1958 GREY CUP CHAMPIONS

FRONT ROW L. to R.: Leo Lewis, Bob Hobert, Roger Savoie, Garland Warren, James Ausley (Manager), Ralph Parliament (President), Buddy Tinsley, Gordon Rowland, Walter Bilicki, Frank Gilliam.

SECOND ROW L. TO R.: Ken Kovacs (Equipment), Russ Lacomy (Equipment), Tony Kehrer, Ed Kotowich, Ron Latourelle, Ted Mikliechuk, Eugene Wlasiuk, Steve Patrick, Herb Gray, Cornel Piper, Jim Van Pelt, Harry "Pop" Varnes (Equipment), Bob Jones (Equipment).

THIRD ROW L. TO R.: Bud Grant (Head Coach), George Druxman, Barry Roseborough, Ernie Pitts, Frank Rigney, Gerry Vincent, Norm Rauhaus, Cec Luning, Wayne Robinson.

BACK ROW L. TO R.: Joe Zaleski (Assistant Coach), Dave Burkholder, Charlie Shepard, Jim Tonn, Keith Pearce, Ken Ploen, Ron Meadmore, John Varone, Nick Miller, Rick Potter.

WINNIPEG BLUE BOMBERS 1959 GREY CUP CHAMPIONS

FRONT ROW L. to R.: Ed Kotowich, Bud Tinsley, Leo Lewis, Cec Luning, Walter Bilicki, Ernie Pitts, Frank Rigney, Nick Miller, Ron Latourelle.

SECOND ROW L. TO R.: Bob Jones (Equipment), Ken Ploen, Gerry James, Norm Rauhaus, Steve Patrick, Herb Gray, Cornel Piper, Charlie Shepard, Gar Warren, Bud Grant (Head Coach).

THIRD ROW L. TO R.: Ken Kovacs (Equipment), Rick Potter, Rae Ross, Tony Kehrer, Ted Mikiliechuk, Jim Van Pelt, Dave Burkholder, Jack Delveaux, Roger Savoie, Carver Shannon, Joe Zaleski (Assistant Coach), George Hills (Vice-President).

BACK ROW L. TO R.: Ralph Parliament (President), Gord Mackie (Trainer), Gordie Rowland, Keith Webster, Ken Bochen, George Druxman, Henry Janzen, Farrell Funston, Ron Meadmore, Jack Bruzell, Pop Varnes (Equipment), John Michaels (Assistant Coach), Jim Ausley (Manager).

WINNIPEG BLUE BOMBERS 1961 GREY CUP CHAMPIONS

FRONT ROW L. to R.: Cornel Piper, Mike Wright, Leo Lewis, Joe Zaleski (Assistant Coach), Bud Grant (Head Coach), John Michaels (Assistant Coach), Nick Miller, Cec Luning, Norm Rauhaus. Insets: Jim Ausley, Gordon Lawson, Barry Manning.

SECOND ROW L. TO R.: Ed Kotowich, Ray Ash, Roger Hamelin, George Druxman, Ted Mikliechuk, Dick Thornton, Jack Delveaux, Steve Patrick, Herb Gray.

THIRD ROW L. TO R.: Jim Thoroski, Roger Savoie, Gord Rsowland, Gerry James, Frank Rigney, Dave Burkholder, Gar Warren, Charlie Shepard, Farrell Funston, Ernie Pitts, Ray Jauch, Gord Mackie (Equipment Manager).

BACK ROW L. TO R.: Frank Fraser, Henry Janzen, Ron Meadmore, Jack Bruzell, Rick Potter, Hal Ledyard, Ken Ploen, Roger Hagberg, Baz Nagle, Rod Homeniuk.

WINNIPEG BLUE BOMBERS 1962 GREY CUP CHAMPIONS

FRONT ROW L. to R.: Roger Savoie, Rod Humenuik, Ernie Pitts, Hal Ledyard, Joe Zaleski (Assistant Coach), Bud Grant (Head Coach), John Michaels (Assistant Coach), Dave Burkholder, Frank Rigney, Leo Lewis, Ron Latourelle.

SECOND ROW L. TO R.: Ray Ash, Roger Hamelin, Cornel Piper, George Druxman, Neil Thomas, Roger Hagberg, Nick Miller, Gar Warren, Steve Patrick, Herb Gray.

THIRD ROW L. TO R.: Bob Jones (Equipment Manager), Farrell Funston, Rick Potter, Henry Janzen, Gord Rowland, Joe Williams, Norm Rauhaus, Gerry James, Gord Mackie (Trainer).

BACK ROW L. TO R.: Cec Luning, Bill Whisler, Sherwyn Thorson, Jack Bruzzel, Charlie Lindsay (Vice-President), Jim Ausley (General Manager), Karl Wintemute (President), Dick Thornton, Jack Delveaux, Ken Ploen, Charlie Shepard.

WINNIPEG BLUE BOMBERS 1984 GREY CUP CHAMPIONS

FRONT ROW L. TO R.: David Shaw, Wylie Turner, John Bonk, Willard Reaves, Mark Moors, Paul Robson (General Manager), Mike Riley, John Gergory, Cal Murphy (Head Coach), Fred Glick, Bob Vespaziani, Art Asselta, Dr. Jan Brown (President), Pat Cantner, Tony Norman, Trevor Kennerd, Bob Cameron, Scott Flagel.

SECOND ROW L. TO R.: Jeep Woolley, Ray Korkiala, Jeff Boyd, Kevin Neiles, James Sykes, Sean Kehoe, John Hufnagel, Tom Clements, John Pitts, Holbert Johnson, Michael Elarms, Ken Hailey, Delbert Fowler, Blair Smith, Kevin O'Donovan, Greg Parker, Pat Clayton.

THIRD ROW L. TO R.: Len Amey, Brian Donak, Nick Bastaja, Frank Robinson, Donovan Rose, Dave Ploughman, Joe Poplawski, Rick House, Jerome Erdman, Todd Hons, Darrell Patterson, Tyrone Jones, James Hood, Rob Majdell, Joe Mack, George Motoch.

BACK ROW L. TO R.: James Murphy, John Sturdivant, Brent Racette, Paul Palma, Richard Nemeth, Stan Mikawos, Doug MacIver, Chris Walby, Val Belcher, Vernon Pahl, James Capers, Norman Gibbs, Aaron Brown, Kevin Hardy.

Photo by Tony Biegun

WINNIPEG BLUE BOMBERS 1988 GREY CUP CHAMPIONS

FRONT ROW L. to R.: Lee Saltz, Trevor Kennerd, Tim Jessie, Bob Cameron, Tom Muecke, Ken Pettway, Cal Murphy (General Manager), Bruce Lemmerman, Bob Padilla, Gene Gaines, Mike Riley (Head Coach), Scott Schuhmann, Urban Bowman, Dr.Ross Brown (President), Rod Hill, Sean Salisbury, James Jefferson III, James Murphy, Perry Tuttle, Tony Johns, Ken Hailey.

SECOND ROW L. TO R.: Kevin O'Donovan, Jeep Wooley, Barb Ledyard, Jean Love, Vicki Czarnecki, Len Amey, Ken Winey, Paul Clatney, Darryl Sampson, Terry Cochrane, Buster Rhymes, Michael Allen, Greg Battle, Dan Wicklum, Bennie Thompson, Darryl Yewchyn, Leon Hatziioannou, David Black, Ross Hodgkinson, Dave Read, Jane Garvie, Bill Quinter, Olive Kostyshyn, Allan Klassen.

THIRD ROW L. TO R.: Karl Loepp, Michael Gray, Aaron Brown, Paul Randolph, James West, Lyle Bauer, Ed McQuarters Jr., Brad Tierney, Chris Walby, Bob Molle, Nick Bastaja, Steve Rodehutskors, Paul Shorten, Jim Grieve.

FOURTH ROW L. TO R.: Delbert Fowler, Randy Fabi, Vernon Paul, Romel Andrews, Stan Mikowos, Willie Fears, Jeff Smith.

Photo by Chill Photographic

WINNIPEG BLUE BOMBERS 1990 GREY CUP CHAMPIONS

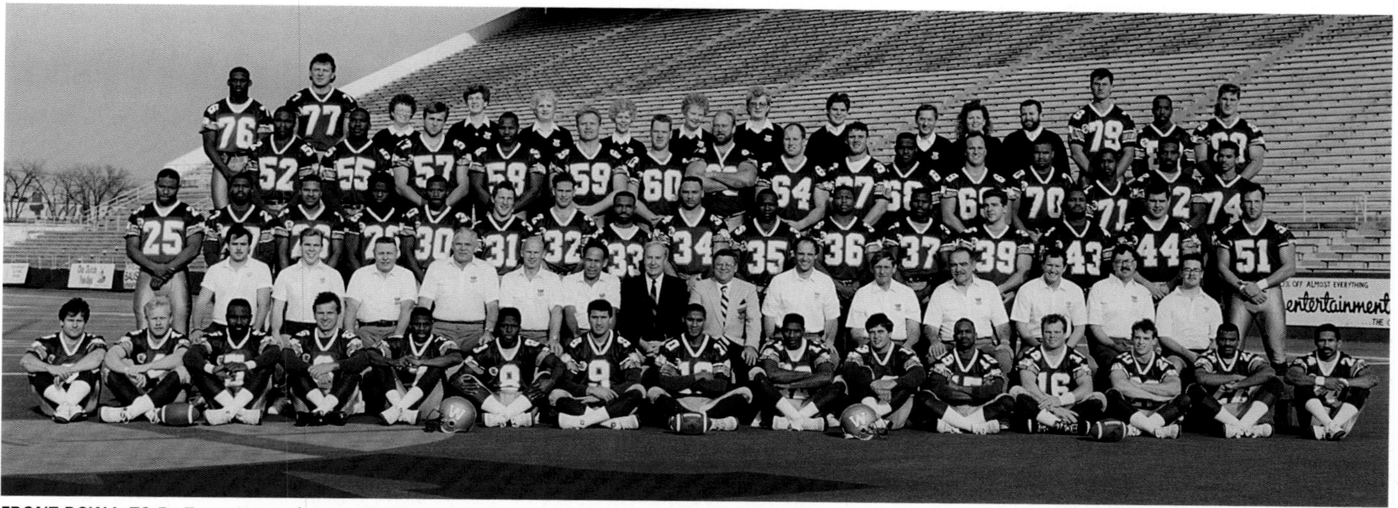

FRONT ROW L. TO R.: Trevor Kennerd, Danny McManus, Tim Jessie, Bob Cameron, Burt Cummings, Ken Pettway, Sammy Garza, Rod Hill, Bobby Evans, Tom Burgess, Less Browne, Terry Cochrane, Steve Zatylny, Perry Tuttle, Ken Hailey.

SECOND ROW L. TO R.: Darren Becker, Jim Grieve, Len Amey, Dave Ritchie, Ron Simonson, Gene Gaines, Cal Murphy (General Manager), Ted Bartman (President), Mike Riley (Head Coach), Jim Gilstrap, Bob Padilla, Scot Maynard, Ross Hodkinson, Sheldon Appelle.

THIRD ROW L. TO R.: Ricky Blake, Robert Mimbs, Ken Winey, Dave Bovell, Darryl Sampson, Rick House, Matt Pearce, Michael Allen, Greg Battle, Tyrone Jones, Paul Randolph, Warren Hudson, John Yule, Quency Williams, Leon Hatziiaonnou, Dave Black.

FOURTH ROW L. TO R.: Mike Gray, Jerome Rinehart, Steve Rodehutskors, James West, Lyle Bauer, Dave Vankoughnett, Chris Walby, Bob Molle, Brian Wise, Nick Benjamin, Scott Redl, David Ward, Lee Hull, Albert Williams, Rodney Hughes.

BACK ROW L. TO R.: Quentin Riggins, Stan Mikawos, Barbara Ledyard, Joyce Murphy, Vicki Czarnecki, Jane Garvie, Jean Love, Olive Kostyshyn, Dave Read, Bill Christie, Dale Bruzell, Kevin O'Donovan, Rob Crifo, Eric Streater, Jeff Croonen. Missing: James Murphy

CanWest: History in the Making

CanWest Global Communications Corp. joins in celebrating the 75th anniversary of the Winnipeg Blue Bombers Football Club, a proud part of Manitoba's history.

Like the Blue Bombers, CanWest is building a legacy in Winnipeg – both on and off the field.

It's been an outstanding road to success on the field for the CanWest team over the last 30 years. Founded and led by the late Israel Asper, the team has seen its share of victories.

It all started in 1974 with the granting of a broadcast licence for a new independent television station in Winnipeg. The station, CKND, now known as Global, launched on September 1, 1975 in a converted grocery store in South Winnipeg, which led to the formation of CanWest Capital, a forerunner to CanWest Global Communications Corp.

The momentum was just starting to build for CanWest and before long Asper had started one of the longest winning streaks in Canadian business history, adding television stations in Eastern and Western Canada, ultimately completing the third cross-Canada network of stations in July of 2000.

In the early 1990s, CanWest established its global game plan and expanded its broadcasting interests, buying television networks in New Zealand and Australia. This paved the way for the purchase of several radio networks in New Zealand and the addition of an out-of-home advertising company to its Australian broadcasting operations, which have proven to be perennial frontrunners in performance and profitability for the CanWest team.

Asper retired as CEO of the company in 1997 to pursue philanthropic interests off the field such as The Canadian Museum for Human Rights project, while remaining Chairman. His son Leonard filled his cleats as President and CEO of CanWest Global Communications Corp. in 1999 and cheers the Bombers on from seats in section D.

CanWest Executive Vice-President and former Bomber Chairman David Asper presents a cheque to Campaign Chair Tom Brick of United Way Winnipeg as the Bombers win the first annual "Banjo Bowl." Part of CanWest's support of the Bombers includes the annual "Banjo Bowl," so named after Bomber kicker Troy Westwood described Saskatchewan football fans as "banjo picking inbreds." The winning team of the annual game between the two prairie clubs receives a $10,000 donation from CanWest to the United Way campaign in the winner's city.

Self-proclaimed 'Bomber fan forever' David Asper remains a driving force behind the powerhouse CanWest team as Executive Vice-President and as a member of the board. He is a former Chairman and current member of the Winnipeg Football Club Board of Directors. He also co-chairs the 2006 Grey Cup Festival in Winnipeg.

Joe Pascucci and Winnipeg Head Coach Cal Murphy on the set of CKND's 'Coach Cal Call In Show' celebrating the Blue Bombers' 1984 Grey Cup Championship.

Other key members of the CanWest team include Israel Asper's wife Babs and daughter Gail, who come up with big returns through their work with The CanWest Global Foundation and The Asper Foundation.

Since its inception 30 years ago, CanWest Global Communications Corp. has become the top team. It has grown to be Canada's leading media company and is Canada's largest publisher of daily newspapers. It owns, operates and holds substantial interests in conventional television, newspapers, out-of-home advertising, specialty cable channels, websites, radio stations and networks in Canada, New Zealand, Australia and Ireland.

Since 1999 CanWest has increased its home team roster nearly tenfold. There are more than 600 employees in Winnipeg with 11,000 employees in total.

Global Television, a major component of CanWest's properties, has been a proud and faithful supporter of the Winnipeg Blue Bombers Football Club for the past 30 years.

A true competitor, Israel Asper built his empire with an unstoppable winning Winnipeg spirit.

"Everything is doable," said Asper. "If you are tenacious enough, you can do whatever you set out to do. Because all you need is more determination than the guys who are trying to stop you."

Go Bombers!

CanWest Global Place

Global TRUE BLUE For 30 Years

On September 1, 2005 Global Television celebrated 30 years of broadcasting in Manitoba. During those 30 years Global (CKND) has been a bomber booster, and sports director Joe Pascucci has many great memories of our home team.

"COACH CAL CALL-IN SHOW"

"The Coach Cal Call-In Show" originated in 1984 as a 30 minute program that gave Bomber fans a chance to phone in and ask questions to Bomber Head Coach Cal Murphy. In 1987, Murphy was replaced by Mike Riley, and the show was re-named "The Big Blue Call-In Show". Blue Bomber fans had the opportunity to voice their opinions for seven years from 1984 to 1990.

"INSIDE THE CFL WITH CHRIS WALBY"

When CKND's "Sportsline" first went on the air in September of 1991, it launched a new Bomber show called "Inside the CFL with Chris Walby." As the CFL insider, Walby would give Sportsline viewers his weekly analysis on the Bombers and other news from around the CFL. This segment became a fan favourite because of the back and forth commentary between Chris Walby and Joe Pascucci. One of their memorable segments was when Walby turned 40, and Pascucci showed photos of Chris wearing a woman's wig at a Bomber party. It was one of the few times that Chris Walby was actually speechless.

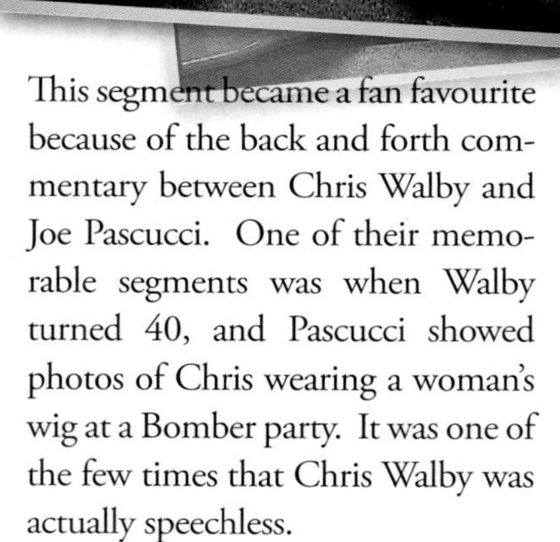

60TH ANNIVERSARY SPECIAL

Global (CKND) has produced a number of Bomber specials over the years. One of the most memorable celebrated the 60th anniver-

sary of the Winnipeg Football Club in 1990. CKND delighted Bomber fans with a trip down memory lane by looking back on many of the great moments in Bomber history.

BLUE AND GOLD 75 YEARS

In June of 2005, Global Television celebrated the Bombers 75th Anniversary season with "Blue and Gold - 75 Years." It celebrated the rich history of the Winnipeg Football Club and also looked ahead to the upcoming CFL season. Head Coach Jim Daley, President and CEO Lyle Bauer, receiver Milt Stegall and running back Charles Roberts all shared their observations on past and future performances. Taped during the club's training camp, the show gave Bomber fans a first look at the 2005 team, and highlighted some of the great players and Grey Cup victories of the past.

GLOBAL'S GAME DAY ANALYST

At every 2005 Bomber home game, one Global Sports' fan will get the opportunity to voice his or her thoughts on the performance of their team. Finally a chance for Bomber fans to have their say on camera. Global's Game Day Analyst will experience a once-in-a-lifetime opportunity by being a sportscaster for a day.

POST GAME REPORT

Blue Bomber fans have come to know that after every Blue Bomber game Global Sports has all the highlights and reactions. Following every home game, Global Sports is LIVE at Canad Inns Stadium with coach and player interviews.

Thanks for the opportunity to bring 30 years of Bomber Action to Viewers and Fans!

CARGILL LIMITED

SUPPORTING AGRICULTURE AND OUR COMMUNITIES FOR OVER 80 YEARS

Cargill applauds the efforts of the **Winnipeg Blue Bombers** organization and its players for not only the high quality entertainment they have given us throughout the years, but more importantly the connection to community in supporting many of the children and families across our province.

Just like the *Blue and Gold,* Cargill has remained an active partner and proud supporter of the communities we have been so privileged to work and live in over the past 80 years.

As we pursue our purpose of being the global leader in nourishing people, we pay close attention to our role as a corporate citizen. How we do business shapes, in important ways, our relationships with employees, customers and the communities in which we do business.

Winnipeg Grain Exchange Building

In particular, Cargill has partnered with a number of organizations through our Cargill Cares program. We remain an active supporter of the United Way, Children's Hospital, Fort Whyte Centre and more recently the Millennium Library – among other centres and projects.

Cargill Canada has grown from a single office in Montreal to a national company headquartered in Winnipeg, Manitoba with over 6,000 employees from Quebec to British Columbia.

In Canada, Cargill is one of the country's largest agricultural merchandisers and processors with interests in chocolate, egg, animal nutrition, malt, fertilizer, meat, natural gas, oilseed processing, salt and starch, as well as crop input products, grain handling and merchandising.

In reflecting upon our growth and many achievements as an industry, I feel compelled to share some of Cargill's past, present, and future.

In 1928, Cargill Grain Company, Limited, was incorporated, and in September of that year, we opened our first office in Montreal, Quebec. Two years later, Cargill took residence in western Canada, by opening our second office in the now well-known Winnipeg Grain Exchange Building.

By the end of World War II, Cargill established a presence in Vancouver, British Columbia to capture opportunities around the anticipated west coast grain movements. Then in 1950, we built our first elevator in Canada, located in Coutts, Alberta, to receive grain from Sweetgrass, Montana, for delivery to Duluth, Minnesota.

Kerry L. Hawkins
President, Cargill Limited

1960 marked a historic benchmark for Cargill Canada with the completion of the largest elevator in the country in Baie Comeau, Quebec. This was the innovation of past president, Cargill Inc., Mr. John MacMillan, Jr. who wanted a terminal at the mouth of the St. Lawrence that would not be iced out during winter.

Not a year later, Cargill Grain partnered with Hannah Mining to create Nipigon Transport Ltd., which

transported grain primarily from the head of the Great Lakes to Baie Comeau.

A memorable step for Cargill Canada was the 1974 purchase of the National Grain Co., Ltd. facilities, as well as inventories from Peavey, consisting of a huge Thunder Bay terminal, 286 country elevators, five feed plants, and one hog farm then, in 1981 Cargill entered the animal nutrition business.

1989 marked a significant transition for Cargill as we diversified further into the meat packing business in High River, Alberta. That same year, we continued our growth in the grain sector with the acquisition of the retail fertilizer distribution network of Cyanamid Canada.

Two years later, Cargill partnered with the Saskatchewan Government to construct Saskferco, one of the largest nitrogen fertilizer plants in the world (now a part of Mosaic).

In 1996, Cargill constructed and began operating Canada's largest canola crushing plant, located just outside Saskatoon, Saskatchewan. And then in 1998, Cargill established itself in the Canadian malting industry with the acquisition of Prairie Malt Limited out of Biggar, Saskatchewan.

In 2002, Cargill purchased Agribrands and along side our animal nutrition operations created a world class animal nutrition company.

January 2002 Cargill proudly entered the chicken business and now operates a processing facility and hatchery in Ontario. Cargill then entered into the chocolate business in June 2002 when it purchased Omnisweet, located in Burlington, Ontario.

Just last year, we became partners in the North American natural gas and electricity trading business through Cargill Power and Gas Markets headquartered in Calgary, Alberta, and in 2004 we acquired Caravelle Foods, an award-winning business that produces frozen beef patties for the Canadian quick service restaurant industry.

All this has led to Cargill's recognition as one of the largest agricultural merchandisers and processors in Canada. It has not been easy, but thankfully all of our employees, suppliers and producers have remained committed to our approach, which is to be trustworthy, creative and enterprising!

Looking ahead, Cargill's success will hinge upon our collective ability to harness our knowledge and energy to provide goods and services that are necessary for life, health, and growth.

So as we approach our **100th Anniversary** in the year 2028, there are bound to be many more changes along the way. I cannot predict the future, but the one thing that I know for certain is that just like the ***Blue and Gold*** the colour of Cargill will become even more connected with the many communities we are so privileged to work in and call home.

Congratulations
Blue Bombers on 75 years!

Winnipeg Free Press

The Winnipeg Free Press has been rolling off the presses since 1872 and in the last 75 years many of those editions chronicled the happenings and helped promote the city's most-famous sports team, the Blue Bombers.

One of the nation's most-respected newspapers and long the voice of Western Canada, The Free Press is only two years younger than the province of Manitoba, which joined Confederation in 1870 and is two years older than the city of Winnipeg itself, which was incorporated in 1874.

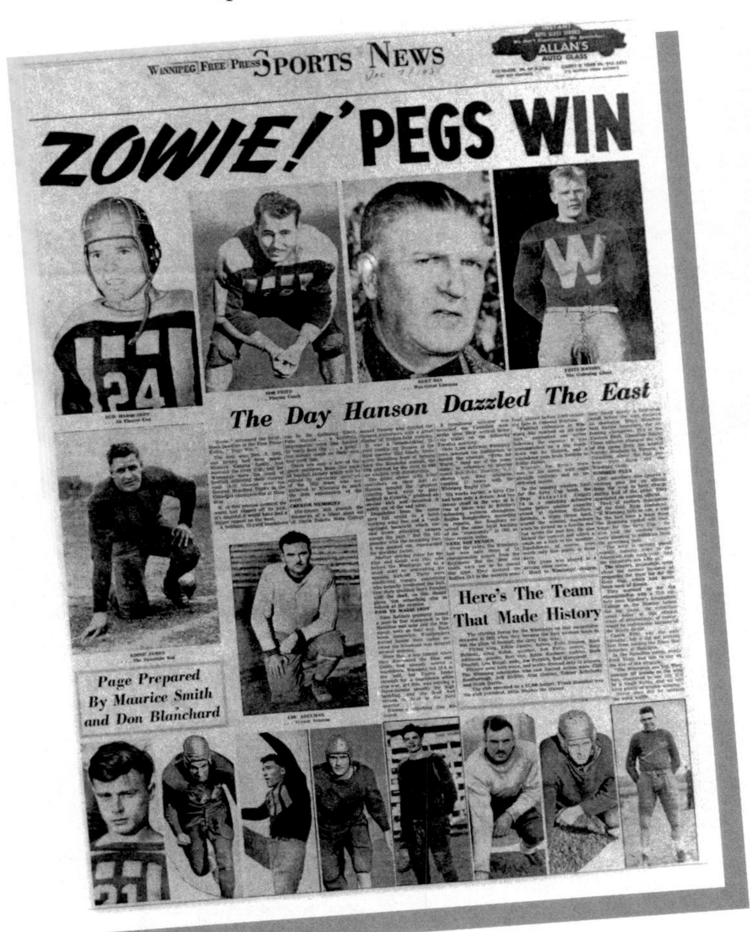

Winnipeg Free Press SPORTS NEWS

ZOWIE! 'PEGS WIN

The Day Hanson Dazzled The East

Here's The Team That Made History

Page Prepared By Maurice Smith and Don Blanchard

As a result, the newspaper has been there not only for the birth of the Blue Bombers, but for the earlier beginnings that laid the foundation for the team's inception. The Free Press was there when the game first became organized in the province with the formation of the Winnipeg Rugby Football Club in 1880. It was there 12 years later when the Manitoba Rugby Football Union hit the ground running with teams like the Victorias, the Winnipeg Rowing Club and the St. John's.

It has been there for every glorious moment in the 75 years of the Blue Bombers, from the day in 1930 when the 'Winnipegs' were formed by Tote Mitchell, through the glory years of Bud Grant, Ken Ploen and Leo Lewis the late 1950s-early 1960s, through the lean years in the 1970s, the three Grey Cups in 1984, 1988 and 1990 and right through to the present.

The newspaper has been there to record the victories and the defeats and the 10 Grey Cup championships. Its writers and editors have helped tell the stories of the team's greatest moments and its greatest players all the while playing a vital role in the franchise's evolution and survival as a corporate sponsor both

Winnipeg Free Press

through the good times and the bad. From its launch some 133 years ago by owner and editor W.F. Luxton and his partner John A. Kenny, The Free Press has grown into the preeminent news source in Winnipeg and the largest selling newspaper in Manitoba.

And just under four years ago in December 2001 The Free Press officially became the largest independent newspaper in Canada when Ronald Stern and Bob Silver – two prominent Winnipeg businessmen with significant local roots – purchased the paper and The Brandon Sun from Thomson Newspapers and established FP Canadian Newspapers Limited Partnership. The Free Press now reaches an average of 126,000 readers seven days a week, including over 173,000 on Saturday. And on those pages the story of this province's storied community-owned football franchise will continue to be told, for The Free Press and the Blue Bombers have been partners for decades and will be for another 75 years – and beyond.

Winnipeg Free Press

Winnipeg Free Press

MANITOBA
BLUE CROSS

CJOB AND THE BLUE BOMBERS,
PART OF MANITOBA'S HISTORY AND HERITAGE

When CJOB went on the air at 8am March 11th, 1946, the Winnipeg Blue Bombers were already 16 years old and well established as a vital part of the community. It didn't take 'OB long to achieve that same distinction. When CJOB took to the airwaves that morning in 1946 from the top floor of the Lindsay building at the corner of Notre Dame and Garry Street with call letters garnered from its founder Jack O. Blick and the motto "Working for Winnipeg", there were two other stations operating in the city at the time, CKY and CKRC.

While CJOB became the first station to broadcast 24 hours a day, the first in Manitoba to provide "News on the Hour-Every Hour" and the first to run "Open Line" shows, along with many other ground-breaking concepts, it took a while before station management embraced the idea of sports coverage and specifically play-by-play.

CKRC and CKY did the radio play-by-play of Bomber games back in those years. It wasn't until the mid 1960s that CJOB decided to plunge head first into the business of in-depth sports coverage. Legendary broadcaster George McCloy did the play-by-play before Bob Picken took over. Cliff Gardiner, one of the biggest Bomber boosters in all of Winnipeg, did a coaches show with Bud Grant before the Silver Fox headed to the Minnesota Vikings.

When Bob Picken left CJOB, Ken "The Friar" Nicolson took over as Sports Director, and he promoted an even more aggressive approach to acquiring play-by-play rights. With Friar doing the call, CJOB broadcast the first ever Winnipeg Jets game in September of 1972. Nicolson found himself doing both Jets and Bomber games in 1974 before turning the football play-by-play over to a fresh young face from Regina, via Brandon, in Bob Irving.

Ever since then, with Irving as the anchor, CJOB has been the radio voice and the radio conscience of the Blue Bombers. Whether it was Jack Matheson on the Football Hotline, pre- and post-game shows from Chi-Chi's Mexican Restaurante, or the familiar voices of Ken Ploen, Mitch Zalnasky, Joe Poplawski, Jack Wells, Geoff Currier, and Roger Currie, CJOB has been with the Bombers through good times and bad, fully appreciating how important the Winnipeg Football Club was, and is, to the culture and history of the city of Winnipeg.

The Blue Bombers and CJOB, linked for decades as two of Winnipeg's proudest and most revered institutions.

From left: Bomber play-by-play voice, Bob Irving with Ken Ploen, "Cactus" Jack Wells and Jack Matheson.

CJOB 68
SUPERSTATION

Manitoba Hydro

Committed to the Community

Manitoba Hydro is committed to being an outstanding corporate citizen. We strive to support organizations like the Winnipeg Blue Bombers, which contribute so much to the vibrancy of our community. On behalf of Manitoba Hydro, congratulations to the Winnipeg Blue Bombers on 75 great years – may there be many more!

Manitoba Hydro is the province's major energy utility. Headquartered in Winnipeg, Manitoba, it provides 505 883 customers with electric energy province-wide. Manitoba Hydro is also the major distributor of natural gas in the province, supplying 253 631 customers in southern Manitoba. Hydro also exports electricity to over 50 electric utilities and marketers in the mid-western U.S., Ontario and Saskatchewan.

A crown corporation, Manitoba Hydro offers its customers a wide range of energy services, either directly or through its subsidiaries. Hydro is also known worldwide for its expertise in high voltage direct current transmission.

Virtually all electricity generated by Manitoba Hydro is from self-renewing water power. On average, about 30 billion kilowatt-hours of electricity are generated annually, with 98 percent produced from 14 hydroelectric generating stations on the Nelson, Winnipeg, Saskatchewan and Laurie rivers.

Manitoba Hydro delivers natural gas throughout southern Manitoba to nearly 100 communities using approximately 8 200 kilometres of pipelines. On average we deliver about 2.1 billion cubic metres of natural gas through our system.

Power Smart*

Power Smart* is Manitoba Hydro's energy conservation strategy. It was designed to help customers use energy more efficiently. Since 1991, up to 600 billion watt-hours in energy have been saved. This is equivalent to running a compact fluorescent light bulb for about 5 million years; heating an average Manitoba home for about 30 000 years, or running the Manitoba Legislature for over 200 years.

The objective of Manitoba Hydro's Power Smart program is to meet energy needs through efficiency improvements rather than through new sources of generation. Savings achieved through conservation measures mean that surplus energy can be exported outside the province. Sales of exported power reduce the price of power charged to Manitobans by as much as 30 per cent, and help to keep Manitoba Hydro's electricity rates among the lowest in North America.

* Manitoba Hydro is a licensee of the Trademark and Official Mark.

Winnipeg Free Press

■ The 'Lincoln Locomotive,' Leo Lewis: *tore through opposition defences for 11 years.*

C O R P O R A T E

CONGRATULATIONS TO THE WINNIPEG BLUE

Winnipeg Free Press

THE
Great-West Life
ASSURANCE COMPANY

A L L - S T A R S

BOMBERS ON 75 YEARS OF GREAT FOOTBALL

MC• LABATT BREWING CO.

A big thank-you to these Winnipeg Blue Bombers corporate sponsors, who also generously supported the production of this book.

ACKNOWLEDGEMENTS

The publishers wish to thank the following individuals and corporations for their valuable assistance in providing photographs and editorial expertise in the production of this book.

Andrea Earl and Rick Brownlee of the Manitoba Sports Hall of Fame & Museum

Peter James, Jude Romualdo and Shandel Happychuk of the Western Canada Pictorial Index

Sharon Foley of the Archives of Manitoba

Marnie Strath and Ken Gigliotti of the Winnipeg Free Press

Brian Hubner, Brett Lougheed, Lewis St. George Stubbs, Michelle Strutt and Shelley Sweeney of the University of Manitoba Archives & Special Collections/Winnipeg Tribune

Jerry Maslowsky of the Winnipeg Blue Bombers

Dave Darichuk

John E. Sokolowski

Charles Shilliday

Trevor Kennerd

John Bradley, Jogo CFL Cards

Friesens

Relish Design Studio Ltd.

and Merv Hart of Brandon, for coming up with the idea.

INDEX